When the Lion Roars Everyone Listens
Scary Good Middle School Social Studies

JEREMIAH CLABOUGH, THOMAS N. TURNER,
KENNETH T. CARANO

D1089361

ASSOCIATION FOR MIDDLE LEVEL EDUCATION

Printed in the United States of America.

ISBN 978-1-56090-287-4

Library of Congress Cataloging-in-Publication Data

Names: Clabough, Jeremiah.
Title: When the lion roars everyone listens : scary good middle school social
    studies / Jeremiah Clabough, Thomas N. Turner, Kenneth T. Carano.
Description: Westerville, Ohio : Association for Middle Level Education,
    [2017] | Includes bibliographical references.
Identifiers: LCCN 2017008503 | ISBN 9781560902874
Subjects: LCSH: Social sciences--Study and teaching (Middle school)--United
    States. | Social sciences--Study and teaching (Middle school)--Activity
    programs.
Classification: LCC H62.5.U5 C623 2017 | DDC 300.71/273--dc23 LC record available
    at https://lccn.loc.gov/2017008503

Association for Middle Level Education
4151 Executive Parkway, Suite 300
Westerville, Ohio 43081 | amle.org

Acknowledgements

We would like to thank Mr. Phillip VanderKamp for opening his classroom to us for some of the activities discussed in this book.

We would like to thank Mrs. Nefertari Yancie for opening her classroom to us for some of the activities discussed in this book.

We would like to thank Mr. Shannon Hamblen for his drawing, which appears in chapter five.

About the Authors

Dr. Jeremiah Clabough is an assistant professor of social science education at the University of Alabama at Birmingham. He is the lead author for *Unpuzzling History with Primary Sources* (2016). His research interests include teaching content area literacy skills with primary sources and graphic novels in middle and high school social studies classrooms.

Dr. Thomas N. Turner has spent 45 years at the University of Tennessee as a social science education professor. He is the author of more than 200 professional articles and several books. His research interests include citizenship education, drama, and writing in the social studies. His next goal is to become a published mystery writer. He has three children and three granddaughters (Tessa, Leia, and Scarlet). All of whom he is very proud of.

Kenneth T. Carano is an associate professor in the division of teacher education with an emphasis in social studies education at Western Oregon University. He is also a returned Peace Corps volunteer who spent two years teaching elementary students and running an after-school program in Suriname. His scholarship interests focus on social justice and global perspectives in teacher education programs and preparing students to be effective citizens in a world that is becoming increasingly interconnected.

Table of Contents

01

Democratizing Social Studies through a Student-Centered Approach

A doctor has to begin with a careful diagnosis before treating a patient's symptoms. Similarly, an effective middle school social studies curriculum must be based on an accurate identification of the learning needs of students. Some of these needs relate to age and stage of development. Others relate to the family and neighborhood; still others are individual and circumstantial. Middle school students are undergoing a great deal of developmental changes. They must be provided with a school curriculum that helps during these life transitions while also challenging them to think critically about their place in the world. The National Council for the Social Studies (NCSS) emphasizes that the ultimate goal is to help prepare students to make positive contributions as citizens in a democratic society (NCSS, 1991). Middle school students need meaningful opportunities to explore the world around them. They should also examine issues related to self-identity as they define their values and beliefs (Roney & Lipka, 2013). Middle school social studies teachers should give careful consideration to the components of their curriculums to allow students to accomplish these goals.

This chapter focuses on a vision for the middle school social studies classroom that uses student-centered instruction. It allows the social studies teacher to meet the evolving needs of students in the 21st century. We will define the components for this type of instruction and make the argument for why traditional didactic teaching is not appropriate to meet students' learning needs. Finally, we will provide an explanation for why student-centered instruction aligns with the goals of the social studies classroom outlined in the Association for Middle Level Education's (AMLE) *This We Believe* (NMSA, 2010) and the position statements of NCSS.

Feeling "Weirder and Weirder" while Wanting to Fit in

Kermit the Frog reminds us that, "It's not easy being green." Likewise, it is not easy being a middle school student. Middle school students simultaneously want to be accepted by their peers but maintain their individuality. They need structure but want independence. The paradoxical nature of students from this age group makes their social interactions with peers and teachers fraught with angst, pressure, uncertainty, and volatility on a daily basis (Brown, 2013). This does not even take into consideration the pressures they face from parents and teachers to academically succeed with more challenging assignments than they were accustomed to in elementary school. Our middle school students often feel twisted into a Gordian knot. They struggle to juggle all of their personal conflicts. Students assume different masks and poses that they feel will improve their image. However, no matter what pose they assume, they feel weird. In other words, "It's complicated." Middle school life may be described as disjointed and discombobulated but that is the way they perceive the world around them.

Middle school students are filled with important questions, serious questions, essential questions, and bizarre questions. The most essential of these has to do with identity- "Who am I?" This question will be defined, redefined, shaped, and reshaped by their choices and actions throughout the rest of their lives because it is an elusive moving target. In the middle school years, many of the puzzle pieces of this question are falling into place. A personal identity is being formed as students grapple with the academic, emotional, social, and cultural realities of becoming a middle schooler (Hawes, Helyer, Herlianto, & Willing, 2013). Students' choices in middle school, therefore, take on greater significance. Many of the choices that students make can have lasting positive and negative outcomes on their lives.

Social studies teachers must be cognizant of this reality as they design classroom activities. Students should be given opportunities to engage in meaningful decision-making experiences. It is not enough that students make choices. They need to defend the reasoning behind their decisions with the use of evidence (Engle & Ochoa, 1988). The thought processes involved in decision making push students out of their comfort zone as they examine the intricacies and possible repercussions of life choices. As students move out of their comfort zone, they increase their ability to make better personal choices and take charge of their own personal lives. The examination of choices is pivotal because of the vast number of changes that students are going through in their middle school years.

Students go through a complex set of emotional, physiological, and social changes during their middle school years (NCSS, 1991). They are starting to develop the ability to do more abstract thinking and are thus very inquisitive about the world around them (Levstik & Barton, 2015). Questions include 1.) How do people influence their government? 2.) Why does this work that way? 3.) How do you know that? These kinds of questions fascinate students who have innate curiosity.

Successful social studies teachers harness students' inquisitive nature with focused planned discussion, careful counseling, and mind-awakening activities. Stimulating students' curiosity should be like opening the flood gates to a dam. Once these flood gates are open, fresh life-giving and life-renewing streams of ideas flow into the classroom. Students should explore life's important questions. These questions lead to a fuller understanding of personal identity and a person's sense of place in society (NCSS, 2013a). They help students learn the relevancy of all of the strange and far away topics of middle school social studies.

The average middle schooler, when asked what happened in school on any day, will shrug and make no comment. This is sad. If we are successfully doing our job, most days students should have vivid positive memories of topics discussed. We believe that what middle school teachers need most are powerful, exciting, student-involving activities--activities that students never forget. These experiences not only teach facts, concepts, and skills but also change attitudes.

People's beliefs, feelings, actions, and inactions should jump off the pages. Our students should be in awe of civil rights activists' suffering to end Jim Crow segregation. They should laugh at the occasional vanity of John Adams as he became jealous of the greater recognition going to Franklin, Washington, and Jefferson. They should weep at the battlefields of the American Civil War, which had become graveyards. The truth is that a strong social studies curriculum evokes emotions (Endacott & Brooks, 2013). Such a curriculum requires a shared vision and focused and flexible planning by middle school teachers and administrators to meet the challenging needs of students in the 21st century (NMSA, 2010).

Avoiding the Venus Fly Trap of "Ground Covering"

The move to a student-centered classroom can be a major shift for some social studies teachers. On the one hand, teachers are pressured by high-stakes national standardized tests on which their students must do well. On the other hand, there are constant societal criticisms of how little students learn. The "No Child Left Behind Era" validated many teachers' natural tendencies to practice what Shirley Engle referred to as "ground covering" in social studies. "Ground covering" is where a teacher feels compelled to cover every chapter in the book and every unit in the school curriculum. This means moving through a great deal of content in a short amount of time (Engle, 1960). If the pacing guide dictates that we are through the War of 1812 by October 1 and we are not, we will rush to catch up by being even shallower in coverage. We may only spend a day on the War of 1812 and two days getting through the presidencies of James Monroe and John Quincy Adams. The focus is on memorizing key terms, accomplishments of historical figures, and a few causes and outcomes of major events.

The "ground covering" approach seems logical to teachers who have to cover a great deal of material before a standardized test. It also makes planning much easier and allows teachers to juggle their many bureaucratic responsibilities. It is almost dictated by the pacing guide and the almighty textbook. Add to that the teachers themselves were primarily taught and trained in this manner. They, therefore, naturally assumed that "ground covering" is the only way to teach social studies.

The problem with this compulsion toward "ground covering" is that it is based on flawed reasoning. Memorized information is not necessarily understood. Covered information does not imply learning. The coverage of topics with "ground covering" prohibits students from exploring topics in depth. They ultimately gain a superficial and shallow understanding of a topic. Historical figures become two dimensional in the minds of our students. Students can answer questions like who was the writer of the Declaration of Independence? However, they struggle with questions like in what ways did Thomas Jefferson shape the educational and political structure of this country? As teachers, we should never be satisfied with our students only being able to answer lower-order questions about our content material.

The use of "ground covering" prevents students from seeing the relevancy of topics to their daily lives. Historical figures are presented in isolation rather than in the context of the period in which they are living. There is no consideration of the reasons for their actions or the impact of these actions. In a "ground covering" approach, George Washington had a plantation named Mount Vernon, fought in two wars, had false teeth, and was the first U.S. President. Then, we move on to other individuals. The topics that we cover in our social studies classroom should have more depth.

This "ground covering" approach ultimately results in fragmented and sporadically connected knowledge of the past. For example, students may connect the outcomes from the Treaty of Versailles in World War I to the origins of World War II. However, they will not figure in the world depression, genocide, and other events that combined to climax in World War II. History is not a thread but a woven tapestry. Events do not happen in isolation but result from multiple causes. Our students need a stronger understanding of topics in social studies if they are to make informed decisions in a democracy.

"Ground covering" disengages students in the learning process. Students become passive. They tune out more than they tune in, producing foggy learning at best. The topics in our disciplines seem irrelevant to their daily lives. Students are more interested in contemporary pop music icons than the U.S. Constitution. This leads to students seeing social studies as just another boring class. Little is learned and even less is expected. Social studies teachers become locked in a struggle against student ambivalence, apathy, and inattention. This type of classroom environment is not conducive to meeting the learning needs of middle school students.

"Ground covering" will not meet the new state and national standards in social studies. The script on what constitutes good teaching in social studies has been flipped over the last couple of years for the most part in a good way. Social studies teachers must actively involve students in the learning process by having them critically analyze a text. This means that they must determine factors such as an author's biases and points of view and summarize the main ideas in a text. All of these skills and processes foster students' higher order thinking skills in social studies (Austin & Thompson, 2015).

 The C3 Framework authored by the National Council for the Social Studies (NCSS) requires social studies teachers to use a variety of teaching strategies to meet the expectations of these standards. Teachers will therefore need to use other approaches than direct instruction for students to successfully meet these new standards (NCSS, 2013b). This is an improvement over the "No Child Left Behind standards" that focused on students memorizing the answers to lower-order questions. The standards in the C3 Framework are more focused on students using analysis skills to examine a historical event. Students must employ the thought processes of social scientists to examine and explore a historical topic (Gilles, Wang, Smith, & Johnson, 2013). The analysis of an issue or event in this manner promotes students' critical thinking skills. This will be a major shift for some social studies teachers. We attempt to include activities to help middle school social studies teachers meet this challenge throughout the chapters of this book. For the activities discussed, example activities are provided, some of which were constructed by middle school students.

Student-Centered
Social Studies Classroom

As authors, we want to offer an alternative to complete reliance on direct instruction. If we can accomplish this, it is reason enough for teachers to read this book. This reasoning is embodied in one of Ben Franklin's assertions about learning. "Tell me and I forget. Teach me and I remember. Involve me and I learn" (Franklin, n.d.). This is consistent with what social studies scholars have said about how students learn (NCSS, 2016). The term that is used to describe this theory is constructivism. Constructivism may be described as students creating new knowledge and understanding by applying background knowledge (Brooks & Brooks, 1999). Constructivist teaching requires a change in the dynamic of the classroom. Students take on a more active role in the classroom while the teacher guides their exploration of topics. Middle school students should never view school as a place where they watch older people work. They need to be actively involved with every step of the learning process.

Our argument is very straightforward. To meet current educational standards, social studies teachers need to use student-centered practices. Students should be actively discussing and exploring the content material in small groups and individually through inquiry-based activities. They then share their findings with the class. The teacher needs to guide and support students' examination of historical texts. This change to the classroom dynamic holds students accountable for their own learning and equips them with the skills to collaborate with others (Wineburg, Martin, & Monte-Sano, 2012). Below are our six components of a student-centered classroom.

1. **Students need to be responsible for their own learning.** We want our students to actively build content-area literacy skills in the social studies through inquiry. Inquiry-based activities build students' research skills as they search for and analyze texts. Social and political groups are constantly

trying to persuade people to support issues, policies, and stances. Friends and family members also want students to make certain decisions on a daily basis. Our students need the ability to weigh and analyze the evidence to make responsible choices throughout their lives (Engle & Ochoa, 1988).

2. **Social studies teachers need to be adaptive and creative.** They do not want to be too reliant on a small set of classroom activities and assessments. Students will be bored with this redundancy, and their learning needs will not be completely met. Our activities and assessments should build upon each other and constantly push students to think at a higher level. They should also allow students to use their own creativity. Teachers need to consider the skill sets of students and use these as the starting point. The difficulty of activities and assessments should incrementally grow in complexity.

3. **The classroom atmosphere should be warm and inviting to all students while at the same time challenging them to think critically.** Students should feel comfortable to voice their opinions and questions. A classroom environment that fosters trust and support is critical if students are going to work collaboratively on classroom activities and assessments with their peers. The teacher should start the semester or school year directly addressing these issues and expectations from the students. All group projects and assignments need to have clearly delineated roles that allow students to be experts on a portion of the content material. This type of learning environment is needed for all students to succeed.

4. **The social studies classroom should be a literacy-based environment.** Teachers need to use a variety of texts within the classroom to promote social studies literacy. These include primary sources, biographies, trade books, and websites related to social studies topics. These sources are vital components to any effective middle school social studies classroom. Students need to be able to use these sources and communicate their understanding of content material found within these texts through writing activities (Nokes, 2013).

5. **Individual identity as a member of a group and as a citizen should be a central focus.** Students are reaching a pivotal point as they enter middle school. They are starting to form a value and belief set about their personal identities and the world around them. Social studies teachers need to design their curriculum to help students find their own voice. Students should explore historical figures' actions and inactions to see repercussions on an individual basis and on a societal level. This examination allows students to see the power that personal choices and decisions can have on a person's life. Through these processes, students also gain an understanding for their responsibilities and duties as a citizen in a democracy. They need opportunities to examine and apply democratic principles in the classroom (Ochoa-Becker, 2007). These kinds of activities help students form a political identity and prepare them for being a democratic citizen.

6. **Students need to develop a world view that allows them to be change agents** (Ochoa-Becker, 2007). To accomplish this goal, social studies teachers should incorporate service-learning projects, collaborative projects that broaden students' vision, and opportunities to experiment with different roles. These types of activities permit students to see the positive influence that they can have on their local and national communities. This gives students the experience of working to better their communities (Butin, 2010). It also prepares them for participation in future community projects.

These six components are reflected in each of the chapters in the book. They are present in both the chapter discussions and in the activities that follow. These discussions and activities are also connected to the 16 characteristics of successful schools described in the Association for Middle Level Education's (AMLE) *This We Believe* (NMSA, 2010).

The Vision of AMLE: *This We Believe*

AMLE sets forth its vision for the middle school classroom in *This We Believe: Keys to Educating Young Adolescents* (NMSA, 2010). The core principles of this book, the position paper of the association, reflect research on the best practices for working with and meeting the learning needs of middle school students. The recommendations provided in *This We Believe* reflect the social, cultural, psychological, and emotional needs of middle school students.

The suggestions are designed to allow middle school teachers and principals to align all aspects of the school to a middle school philosophy. Teachers are provided guidance on structuring their classroom activities to promote higher order thinking and to using assessments that measure learning. AMLE also suggests recommendations for administrators on creating a school-wide environment that supports and nurtures all students. The 16 characteristics proffered in *This We Believe* are steeped in the literature about the unique needs of students in the middle school years.

Connecting *This We Believe* to the Social Studies

In developing an approach to the social studies, our goal is to capture the essence of the middle school philosophy that is articulated in AMLE's *This We Believe* by reflecting that philosophy in the discussions, classroom activities, and assessments in each chapter. *This We Believe* presents 16 characteristics of effective middle schools, divided in the categories of "Leadership and Organization," "Culture and Community," and "Curriculum, Instruction, and Assessment."

The emphasis on a middle school social studies classroom by its very nature requires that we primarily focus on "Curriculum, Instruction, and Assessment." Therefore, the activities and assessments in our chapters are designed to be meaningful, engaging, and interdisciplinary. These qualities for activities and assessments are crucial for a social studies classroom if students are to explore the content material in depth and understand the relevancy of it to their daily lives. Our goal is to help middle school social studies teachers in their quest to align their classrooms with the goals and aspirations of AMLE's *This We Believe*.

Conclusion

Social studies instruction has undergone major changes over the last couple of years. The shift away from direct instruction with an emphasis on "ground covering" to a student-centered classroom brings major changes for social studies teachers. However, this change is not a bad thing; in fact, it is an opportunity to better help meet the learning needs of students and successfully achieve the new education reform standards. The education reform standards found in the C3 Framework reflect best practices outlined in AMLE's *This We Believe* (NMSA, 2010). We have laid out key components of our student-centered classroom in this chapter and connected it to the essential characteristics of *This We Believe*.

To be effective, middle school social studies teachers must captivate and spark the curiosity of students. Students must be able to see the relevance of content material covered to their daily lives. Middle school social studies teachers need to be able to recognize, adapt, create, and implement classroom activities and assessments that make historical figures and their values three dimensional in the minds of students. Such activities should be powerful enough that they become lifetime positive memories for students. Such memories can help shape their lives positively. Our goal with this book is to model classroom activities and assessments to accomplish these goals while at the same time helping develop within our students the necessary skills and dispositions to succeed in the 21st century.

References

Austin, H. & Thompson, K. (2015). *Examining the evidence: Seven strategies for teaching with primary sources.* North Mankato, MN: Maupin House Publishing.

Brooks, J. & Brooks, M. (1999). In search of understanding: The case for constructivist classrooms (2nd ed.). Alexandria, VA: ASCD.

Brown, D. (2013). Developing caring, humanistic classrooms: Effects on young adolescents' complete growth. In K. Roney & R. Lipka (Eds.), *Middle grades curriculum: Voices and visions of the self-enhancing school* (17-31). Charlotte, NC: Information Age Publishing.

Butin, D. (2010). *Service-learning in theory and practice.* New York, NY: Palgrave Macmillan.

Endacott, J. & Brooks, S. (2013). An updated theoretical and practical model for promoting historical empathy. *Social Studies Research and Practice, 8*(1), 41-57.

Engle, S. (1960). Decision making: The heart of the social studies. *Social Education, 24*(7), 301–306.

Engle, S. & Ochoa, A. (1988). *Education for democratic citizenship: Decision making in the social studies.* New York, NY: Teachers College Press.

Franklin, B. (n.d.). Retrieved from http://www.americanhistorycentral.com/entry.php?rec=469&view=quotes.

Gilles, C., Wang, Y., Smith, J., & D. Johnson. (2013). "I'm no longer just teaching history." Professional development for teaching Common Core State Standards for literacy in social studies. *Middle School Journal, 44*(3), 34–42.

Hawes, D., Helyer, R., Herlianto, E., & Willing, J. (2013). Borderline personality features and implicit shame-prone self-concept in middle childhood and early adolescence. *Journal Clinical Childhood Adolescent Psychology, 42*(3), 302-8.

Levstik, L. & Barton, K. (2015). *Doing history: Investigating with elementary and middle schools* (5th ed.), New York, NY: Routledge.

National Middle School Association [NMSA]. (2010). *This we believe: Keys to educating young adolescents.* Westerville, OH: Author.

National Council for the Social Studies [NCSS]. (1991). *Social studies in the middle school.* Retrieved from http://www.socialstudies.org/positions/middleschool.

NCSS (2013a). *Revitalizing civic learning in our schools.* Retrieved from http://www.socialstudies.org/positions/revitalizing_civic_learning.

NCSS. (2013b). *The college, career, and civic life (C3) framework for social studies state standards: Guidance for enhancing the rigor of K-12 civics, economics, geography, and history.* Retrieved from http://socialstudies.org/c3.

NCSS. (2016). A vision of powerful teaching and learning in social studies. *Social Education, 80*(3), 180-182.

Nokes, J. (2013). *Building students' historical literacies: Learning to read and reason with historical texts and evidence.* New York, NY: Routledge.

Ochoa-Becker, A. (2007). *Democratic education for social studies: An issues-centered decision making curriculum.* Charlotte, NC: Information Age Publishing.

Roney, K. & Lipka, R. (2013). Introduction: The vision. In K. Roney & R. Lipka (Eds.), *Middle grades curriculum: Voices and visions of the self-enhancing school* (xiii-xxiii). Charlotte, NC: Information Age Publishing.

Wineburg, S., Martin, D., & Monte-Sano, C. (2012). *Reading like a historian: Teaching literacy in middle and high school history classrooms.* New York, NY: Teachers College Press.

02

Discovering and Nurturing the Inquiring Spirit of Middle Schoolers

In *This We Believe: Keys to Educating Young Adolescents*, the position paper of AMLE (NMSA, 2010), we are reminded that learning "the right answers" is not enough for contemporary society. Middle school students must be empowered to be "successful in a global society." This means that students have to become lifelong learners who are able to "apply sophisticated skills in a variety of situations and to solve complex problems individually and in collaboration with others."

The approach to learning that best fits this description is called inquiry. In this chapter, we will look at the importance that inquiry can have in social studies at the middle school level, describe some of the salient features of inquiry, and speak to the development of key inquiry skills. These skills include questioning, hypotheses-making, and drawing conclusions. We also suggest a typology for inquiry. Finally, we will share a series of classroom strategies based on this typology.

The Essential Features of Inquiry

Martin-Hansen (2002) describes the essential features of inquiry as engaging the learner in scientifically-oriented questions, giving priority to evidence in responding to these questions, formulating explanations based on the evidence, connecting explanations to existing knowledge, and reconciling the explanations to existing knowledge. Stephenson (2007) looks at inquiry from the learners' points of view. He argues that inquiry involves learners in a series of processes, which we have adapted below:

- Tackling real-world questions, issues, and controversies
- Developing questioning, research, and communication skills
- Solving problems or creating solutions
- Collaborating within and beyond the classroom
- Developing deep understanding of content knowledge
- Participating in the public creation and improvement of ideas and knowledge (Stephenson, 2007, p. 1)

Inquiry, once begun, is like an avalanche, growing in size, momentum, and power into something mighty and unstoppable.

The best working definition of inquiry has to be based on the critical elements of the process. However, a list of these elements should not be seen as a series of distinctive individual steps. Rather, the analogy that seems most apt is that of a musical melody line mixed with an occasional chord. Each element is a different note on the scale. The melody line leaps back and forth on that scale. Here then are some of the identifiable elements from the authors' perspectives:

- Developing skills in planning and asking insightful, probing questions.

- Shifting the role of the teacher from being the major knowledge provider to being a guide.

- Developing sensitivity to problems along with the ability to clearly describe and identify them.

- Acquiring skills in hunting for, identifying, and weighing and evaluating information for relevancy, importance, accuracy, and pattern.

- Building the ability to compare, contrast, and reconcile new learning with past knowledge.

- Finding alternative sources to corroborate or contradict hypotheses.

- Developing the ability to weigh and compare competing hypotheses.

The soul of inquiry is insatiable, intellectual curiosity. That curiosity, in turn, inspires a need to ask questions and solve problems and the unstoppable desire to discover answers and solutions for them. The questions and problems themselves create an ache for better questions and clearer definitions of the problems. At that point, the entire process is so ingrained, fundamental, and strong that there is no force on Earth that can stand in its way. Now if that is not what we want our middle schools to do for our students, what is?

Better Questions and Better Questioning Strategies

This We Believe (NMSA, 2010) notes that the "Changes in the patterns of thinking become evident in the ideas and questions that middle school students ask about the world and how it functions." AMLE goes on to point out the importance of the questions students pose to each other and to trusted adults. The teacher's role is not to be merely a sounding board but to help guide the students. The truth is that middle level students need to be taught how to ask questions that move inquiry forward efficiently and purposefully. This is neither easy to accomplish nor quickly achieved. It takes time and planning. To use questions as a learning tool, students need to develop new skills and more analytical ways of thinking.

To become efficient, effective questioners, students need to ask questions that are imaginative and move the inquiry forward. We believe that good questioning strategies have at least five features. The first three of these have to do with the individual questions themselves being appropriate, relevant, and important. All three qualities have to be present in each and every question. The fourth and fifth features involve how the questions relate to one another. Good questioning strategists focus all of their questions on a single purposeful direction and that focus becomes increasingly narrow.

One major precept of questioning is that questioning strategies need to be thought out and prepared in advance. This does not mean that there is no room for spur of the moment impromptu questioning. Inspiration is an essential part of a good questioner's portfolio of skills. Even so, impromptu questions are best formed when the inquirer has filled up his or her mind with information and ideas and something serendipitous that the questioner comes upon triggers a new line of inquiry.

Inquiry as Prophecy: Becoming a Good Guesser

Students often find it hard to understand exactly what a hypothesis is. In *How We Think*, the great American educational philosopher, John Dewey, made the curious and oft quoted statement, "A problem well put is half-solved" (Dewey, 1910, p.2). Among the conclusions that can be reached from reading Dewey is that guessing, or drawing hypothetical conclusions to be examined, is an important, if not essential part of the inquiry process. However, Dewey does not want us to limit ourselves to a few hypotheses. He suggests making good guesses, making lots of guesses, making many of these guesses as wild and unusual as possible, and then deferring judgment and decision making until you have as much information and data as possible. The better an inquirer becomes at hypothetical thinking the more likely he or she is to consider all possible solutions to a problem, even the most unlikely.

Skill in hypotheses making requires combining prior knowledge, personal experience, broad understanding of how things work, logic, intuition, and openness to serendipity. Practice helps. There is also an element of chance or luck that enters into the picture, whether scientists want to admit it or not. The best hypothesis makers plug in time and effort to the formula. This includes a constant examining of evidence and past experience.

To help us understand one way that this works, let us look at an example. Suppose I want to know why some urban areas have grown rapidly and regularly while others have grown sporadically or not at all. I might hypothesize that transportation was a factor and look for major railroad lines, highway crossings, and locations where cities are on rivers or are major ports. Other possible factors might be natural resources in the area, events in history like gold strikes, and manufacturing plants being founded. Another source of hypotheses might be to look at analogies like fads and trends or the transforming power of inventions. Looking at individual cities in order to examine how their history has affected their growth might help identify some possibilities. Factors such as climate and inventions (air conditioning or faster and cheaper travel) should also be considered. Somewhere in the process, I might particularly attune myself to making far-fetched guesses like sudden climate change and increases in early retirement or life expectancy.

The "Smoke and Mirrors" of Inquiry

Inquiry is both problem centered and evidence based. This dovetails beautifully with several of the goals of middle level education as outlined in *This We Believe* (NMSA, 2010). These goals include developing the abilities to think rationally, to ask relevant and significant questions, to independently gather, access, and interpret information, and to use digital tools to explore, communicate, and elaborate. Not coincidently this dovetails with the vision shared by the National Council for the Social Studies (NCSS) in its C3 Framework related to inquiry-based teaching (NCSS, 2013).

Inquiry is not a simple process. Inquiry means living in that uncomfortable space where we do not know the answers (Quillen, 2013). There are definitive elements in inquiry that may be identified and, to some degree, described. However, to try to find a single consistent order in which these elements may be arranged to solve problems is like trying to organize smoke. Any attempt to teach such an order to middle school students only impedes their understanding.

That was exactly what many social science teachers did in the 1970s and 1980s (Washington & Dahlgren, 2010). They pulled a rigid structure from even older literature that they labeled "the scientific method" and attempted to lever it in to fit all problems. By the 1970s, there was considerable conflict in the social studies field about both what teachers were to teach and how to teach. There was the "old history" camp advocating coverage of content, largely textbook based, and the new history camp, which advocated social science approaches (Evans, 2004).

There was an apathy toward social studies that had leaders like McTygue comment on the reduction of social studies in the schools, that neither teachers nor students were "doing history." There was also a general apathy for social studies (Fiensterwal, 2015). Ravitch (2015) commented that history has been "submerged into social studies." She went on to say that we have gotten to a point where all you need to do is be able to keep a few pages ahead of the students in the history text to be a history teacher. She claimed that one of the nation's greatest needs was "well prepared teachers 'who love history' and know enough about it to awaken students' interest and get them to read more than the textbooks." While a schema of ordered steps may not be practical, it may be useful to consider a set of possible inquiry models. One way of looking at this is to offer a possible classification of inquiry approaches based on how much guidance and structure are given and who is doing the guiding and structuring. Martin-Hansen (2002) developed one such categorization of different types of inquiry. This invoked us to rethink the matter and suggest our own typology of models as depicted in the following chart (Figure 2.1).

Figure 2.1 *Typology of Inquiry*

Type of Inquiry	Sub-type	Kinds of Questioning Strategies	Stage	Stage
Closed Inquiry	Teacher Directed	Teacher Guided	Correct Answers	Teacher Guided
	Student Directed	Student Determined	Correct Answers	Teacher Guided
Directed Structured Open Inquiry	Data Driven	Teacher Guided	Possible, Acceptable Answers	Teacher Guided
	Values Loaded	Teacher Guided	Possible, Answers	Teacher Guided

Figure 2.1 (continued) *Typology of Inquiry*

Guided Structured Open Inquiry	Data Driven	Teacher Guided	Possible, Acceptable Answers	Teacher Guided
	Values Loaded	Teacher Guided	Possible, Answers	Teacher Guided
Structured Open Inquiry		Focused on Data	Data Relevant	Teacher Selected Open Choice
Group Directed Inquiry		Group Structured, Teacher Consulted	Group Determined	Group Selected and Teacher Recommended
Individually Directed Inquiry		Student Structured, Teacher Consulted	Individually Determined	Individually Selected and Teacher Recommended

These proposed models provide one way of looking at different types of inquiry. The National Council for the Social Studies (NCSS) position statement entitled "Powerful Teaching" posits that social studies teaching and learning are powerful when they are meaningful, integrative, values based, challenging, and active (NCSS, 2016). All of the models are steeped in these qualities. In the remaining sections of this chapter, we provide an activity for each of these six types of inquiry.

Closed Inquiry: Lincoln's Generals

Closed inquiry begins with a problem created or offered by the teacher. The teacher also structures a series of questions or points that lead the students toward a verifiable correct solution. This type of inquiry allows students to focus on the methods of research and gives them a sense of satisfaction after reaching observable success.

Present the following scenario to the students. Abraham Lincoln from the very first day of his presidency found the nation on the brink of a civil war. What is more, he was faced with the resignation of many of his most competent and brilliant officers because of their commitment to the Confederacy and their own home states. As a result, Lincoln struggled throughout the war to find generals capable enough to turn the tide of battle and bring Union victory.

Now the President has called on you to advise him on the decision about who will command the army. Realizing that nicknames are sometimes realistic and sometimes sarcastic indicators of how the soldiers feel about their officers, you first look at a list of officers' nicknames to see if any of them tell you anything. See Figure 2.2 for a list of Union generals.

Figure 2.2 *Real Nicknames of Union Generals*

The Boy General	Old Goggle Eyes	Kill Calvary
Old Buck	Fighting Joe	Black Jack
The Butcher of Kentucky	Unconditional Surrender	Young Napoleon
Beast	Old Common Sense	The War Eagle
Old Brick Top	Sledge	Old Stars
The Gray Wolf	Speculator	Perpetual Punisher
Old Brains	Uncle Billy	Doc
The Pathfinder	Little Phil	The Great Decliner
	Old Fuss and Feathers	The Hound

Based on nicknames alone, choose five that you might consider to be the commanding general of the Union army. You can find the identities of these generals at *http://www.ageod-forum.com/showthread.php?5682-Union-Generals-Nicknames*. Of course, you realize that this is really an inadequate basis of looking at possible candidates. Therefore, it is important to look in more depth at the officers.

At this point, the teacher needs to arrange the students in small groups to look at the following descriptions of generals (Figure 2.3) in order to make their final recommendations about who would be best to command the Army of the Potomac (the main Union army in the East). Hand out a set of brief descriptions of generals similar to the following one. Do not identify the names of those on the list. Have the groups discuss these and make a rank ordered recommendation to President Lincoln. All of these men actually commanded the Army of the Potomac at one time during the war.

Figure 2.3 *Real Nicknames of Union Generals*

General #1:	This general is an experienced career soldier and a civil engineer who designed a network of lighthouses. He has served in several major battles with distinction and success. This general was severely wounded in one. He is particularly talented at fighting defensive battles. His one flaw is that his record is one of inconclusive campaigns where he fails to follow up.
General #2:	This general is very capable in organizing and training troops, as well as meticulous in planning and operations. He continually overestimates the strength of his opponents and has a tendency to leave a large part of his own command unengaged. This officer may lack the ability to handle an aggressive enemy in a fast moving battle.
General #3:	This general has served successfully in the West commanding in several victories of great strategic importance. He is known to be very aggressive. This officer incorporated African American slaves into the army. His critics claim that he tends to win by brute force rather than superior strategy.
General #4:	This general has served mostly as a staff officer, never as a field commander. He was an aide to General Wool during the Mexican War. This general has just been promoted to Brigadier General. He does not want the job and feels he does not have the right expertise. This officer is imaginative and complex in planning strategies but does not always take into account the capabilities of the soldiers under his command.

General #5:	This general has distinguished himself as an aggressive and audacious commander. He has served in the Mexican War and the Seminole Wars and distinguished himself leading the initial attacks at Antietam. This general has been known to conspire against and be critical of his own commanders. Some worry that he might lose his nerve against a superior commander.
General #6:	This general served in the Mexican War and has training as both an artillery officer and cavalry strategies. Between the wars, he has developed and manufactured a carbine rifle and equipped a large portion of the U.S. Cavalry with the weapon. Bad investments led him to bankruptcy, and he then worked as Illinois Central Railroad treasurer. He was successful at raising volunteers at the beginning of the war and in training. This general served in several major battles of the U.S. Civil War. He has had limited success and been accused of being too cautious.

After the groups have shared their recommendations, you can reveal who the descriptions refer to and tell them that all of these men were given the command at different times. Sharing a timeline of the service of these and others may also help. One is found online at: *http://www. timeforhistory.net/HistoricalInformationPageImages/AmericanCivilWar/ ACWLincolnPicksHisGeneral/AmericanCivilWarGeneralsInTheUnionArmy. html* The commanders are as follows: #1. Meade; #2. McClellan; #3. Grant; #4. McDowell; # 5. Hooker; #6. Burnside. (See also: *https://en.wikipedia.org/wiki/ List_of_American_Civil_War_generals.*)

If you follow up the students' decisions with a timeline of the war, you can see the relative effectiveness of each general. The activity shows the difficulty of making such decisions and that the past does not always predict the future but usually does. More importantly, students gain experience by making historical decisions, which helps them make informed and responsible life choices (NMSA, 2010). This introduces students to closed inquiry in which there are verifiable answers.

⬤ ACTIVITY Directed, Structured Open Inquiry: Investment Decisions

In this type of inquiry, we are looking for possible acceptable answers rather than correct ones. The teacher serves as guide and selects the problems, which students struggle to solve. Often, solving the problem is based on both data and values (Engle, 1960). This teaches students the importance of values in life decisions.

Again, we begin with a scenario, this one looking 25 years into the future. You have worked hard for several years at this point. Through watching how you spend, carefully saving all of the money that you could, and investing it carefully, you have accumulated slightly over $100,000. You suddenly become aware of an opportunity to invest your savings in a way that may give you a big return in a relatively short time. A brilliant friend of yours is starting a new company. This company has the technology and creativity to develop a new type of home video game that will create a holodeck multisensory experience similar to the one envisioned in *Star Trek: The Next Generation*. The company has already written a large number of excellent storylines and scenarios that really impress you. Their graphics are far and above any that you have seen up to now.

This company needs money for production, marketing, and distribution. It is willing to give you a sizable portion of the company's stock in order to have the capital needed. There is a catch though; you will need to chip in your entire savings in order to give the company a proper start up. Remember, this is speculative, and you might lose it all, so you want to be careful. A tour of the facilities and meeting with the people in creation, production, distribution, and marketing has been impressive. You have asked for and gotten an opportunity to meet with management for a final round of questions before you commit.

Now what is needed is a plan for the questions to be asked in that meeting. Both substance and tone are going to be important. Plan at least two questions from each of the categories below:

- Questions about the company itself

- Question about what your role in the company will be and especially what part you will play in decision-making

- Questions about the market

- Questions about key personnel and their contracts

- Questions about the competition

- Questions about record keeping and accounting

Going through this planning process will teach students to consider all factors in solving a problem and to ask better questions in a structured way. This might be a good opportunity to get students to think more carefully about question words like the "5 W's." According to *This We Believe*, the ability to formulate and answer questions is an important life skill that should be worked into a social studies curriculum (NMSA, 2010). It should also help students realize that single questions need to be part of a carefully planned strategy.

Guided, Structured Open Inquiry: Freedom and the Bill of Rights

In this form of inquiry, we seek all of the possible acceptable answers. The teacher structures the process for efficiency and serves as a guide. This kind of inquiry teaches students not to stop with obvious solutions to a problem but to seek elegant and unusual solutions.

Make sure that the students have some background on the Bill of Rights. Part of this is learning about how the first ten amendments of the Constitution were designed more to complete the Constitution than to change it. Without giving students the opportunity to directly refer to the Bill of Rights, present them with a list of possible rights similar to the following and have them add any other "rights" that they might think to be of importance.

- Free speech
- Freedom from imprisonment without cause
- Right to a trial by jury if you are accused of a crime
- Freedom to get together with friends
- Right to own property
- Right to vote
- Right to run for and hold office
- Right to do what you want when you want to do it
- Right to go to church of your choice or not go at all
- Protection of your property and life
- Right to own weapons
- Right to defend yourself
- Right to drive
- Right to surf the Internet
- Right to write what you want on the Internet
- Right to use any words you want
- Right to stay out as late as you want

- Right to wear whatever clothing you want to wear

- Right to wear as little clothing as you want to wear

- The right to dance

Have students discuss these rights, guiding them to ask evaluative questions. After sufficient discussion, divide the students into groups and have them select ten of the rights that they think are most important. Afterwards, discuss their dilemmas, compare the choices of different groups, and examine their choices against the actual Bill of Rights.

This activity shows that priorities play an important role in life decisions. We have many things that we want to do with our time, money, and resources, but insufficient amounts of these three force us to choose what is most important, useful, and of the greatest value. It also teaches students that every decision has consequences, both good and bad. With this activity, the teacher helps support students in the processes that come with making a decision (NMSA, 2010).

 **Structured Open Inquiry: Landing and Survival of the Pilgrims**

Structured open inquiry is focused on finding data that is relevant to important questions. The teacher guides the students in both the selection of problems and their research methods. The goal is to help students do better in both of these. Therefore, the teacher needs to withhold expertise to allow students the greatest independence possible.

Ask the students to consider the following complex interrelated questions. "Did the founders of Plymouth Plantation bring sufficient provisions for their survival as a colony? This plantation later came to be known as Massachusetts. If so, why did so many die in the first few years? If not, what possible reasons can you think of for their lack of supplies?"

This is an activity for students to search for and identify the relevance and importance of possible causes contributing to a historical event. Begin with a possible outcomes discussion, brainstorming a possible contributing factor to the situation that the Pilgrims or "Strangers" were faced with in the early years of the colony, the ways in which they coped, and the impact of weather and circumstance. A timeline from the beginning of the voyage of the Mayflower and the Speedwell may be of some help here.

At the end of the discussion, divide the students into two groups. One group will try to find evidence that the Pilgrims should have planned for and prepared for the situation better. The other group will try to find support for the idea that the expedition encountered circumstances that would have been impossible to anticipate. The resources cited in the following section should help both groups.

Resources for the Activity

- Bradford, W. (2006). *Of Plymouth Plantation 1620 to 1647.* Mineola, NY: Dover Books.

- Cross-Sections of the Mayflower. (n.d.). *Retrieved from http://www. newnorth.net/~johhnson/geneology/mayflower.html.*

- Immigrant Ships Transcribers' Guild: The Mayflower (2015). Retrieved from *http://immigrantships.net/newcompass/ships/ship_files/mayflower.html.*

- Mayflower History.com. (2013). Retrieved from *http://mayflowerhistory.com.*

- Plymouth Plantation. (2015). Retrieved from *http://www.plimoth.org/?gclid =CIXkxpyv5cYCFQYoaQodspoOsQ*.

- World History Project (2015). Plymouth Colony timeline. Retrieved from *https://worldhistoryproject.org/topics/plymouth-colony*

This activity enables students to look at the consequences of decision making. It also allows them to look at multiple causations and to the difficulty of planning for every eventuality. This allows students to see the connections among events in our social studies curriculum (NMSA, 2010). An additional benefit with this type of inquiry is that it teaches how essential having complete data can be in solving problems.

Group Directed Inquiry: The Glory that Was Greece

In this type of inquiry, students in groups make practically all of the decisions. They choose the topic of inquiry, pose the questions, make hypotheses, and do the research. The teacher serves only as a consultant. This moves students toward independent problem solving and thinking. It also helps them work cooperatively.

This inquiry activity is set up for a unit on Ancient Greece. Students work in groups of four to make decisions about the nature of the inquiry, its subject, and the methods. Group member roles are determined by the group. One suggested role set is: leader, recorder, evaluator/reporter, and editor. Each group should meet with the teacher at least four times at checkpoints. The scheduling of these checkpoints, set by the teacher, provide deadlines to keep the activity on schedule. At the first meeting of the group, students choose one of the areas of inquiry (Figure 2.4). If they go off-book and identify an unlisted area, the teacher must approve it.

Figure 2.4 *Possible Areas of Inquiry with Ancient Greece*

The Birth of Democracy in Athens The Spartan Way of Life Building and Sculpture Greek Myths and Legends Law Codes of Solon and Lycurgus Ostracism Greek Theatre	Alexander the Great Greek Philosophers The Trojan War The Sea and Trade Religion and the Olympic Gods Greek Slavery—The Helot System

The students will do the research in designated checkpoints.

Checkpoint 1: Prior to checkpoint 1, the groups should have made a choice about their particular area of inquiry. Make sure that no two groups have selected the same topic. Each group should discuss its area in broad terms. The groups might start by posing several alternative inquiry questions to pursue. The teacher will help them choose the questions with the best potential and begin planning the next phase.

Checkpoint 2: Prior to the meeting with the teacher, the groups need to be gathering and selecting resources. They should have "Googled" the topic using at least three different search words or phrases, printed up a few pages of each of the search results, and checked off the most likely sources on these pages. The group also should have consulted with the librarian for print resources that are available and selected at least four of these for use. In the checkpoint discussion, the teacher can help with recommendations about the various sources and help further refine the inquiry question.

Checkpoint 3: At this point, the groups should have begun to determine hypotheses and have four or more proposed hypotheses ready. These need to be discussed with the teacher to help refine the inquiry. Discussions should include references to information obtained from the resources. Suggestions for additional research to find corroborating sources can be made and planning should be initiated for the synthesis presentation.

Checkpoint 4: Prior to this checkpoint, the teacher should create and share a rubric for evaluating the presentation. This checkpoint should focus on pulling the inquiry together, looking back over what various group members have discovered, and planning for a presentation. This may be a narrated PowerPoint with each group member making contributions, a scripted drama, an art project, a mock trial, or some other form altogether.

In This We Believe, AMLE (2010) points out the need for middle schoolers to work together to make cooperative decisions. The ability to do this well is important to adults. This activity encourages group planning, division of labor, and group decision making. The checkpoints in this activity are key reminders of having a planned order for inquiry and of the necessity in life of working on a timeline.

 ## Individually Directed Inquiry: The Nation Begins

This type of inquiry encourages independent thinking and initiative. The teacher again serves only as a consultant, but this role is intensified by the fact that every student needs that advice. One key advantage is that student individual interests are being addressed. The teacher consultation includes a great deal of motivational counseling as well as helping find resources suitable for students. Once students' interests are unlocked, inquiry is unstoppable and unending.

Have students begin this activity by looking through a list of people from the period in American history beginning in the pre-Revolutionary years up through the early 1800s (see Figure 2.5). Each student needs to select two or three possible individuals to examine more closely and look those up on the Internet. Their initial activity is to use key terms to search the

Internet for the purpose of choosing one individual as a focus. "Googling" is a familiar term for middle schoolers, but the teacher does need to help them search better. Suggest the following criteria to help guide selection:

- The individual you choose should have had a significant role in American history.

- You need to look for a person about whom many primary sources are available including some quotes.

- Your choice should be someone you are curious about, someone with whom you might enjoy conversing.

Figure 2.5 *List of Possibilities*

George Washington Thomas Jefferson Benjamin Franklin John Adams Abigail Adams Paul Revere	John Hancock Nathanael Greene Daniel Boone Molly Pitcher Betsy Ross Phyllis Wheatley	William Howe Lord Charles Cornwallis Henry Knox Gouverneur Morris George Rogers Clark

It will not matter whether more than one student chooses the same figure since their final products will be unique.

After choosing their focus of inquiry, students will create a script for a dramatized pretend interview. To do this, they will need to prepare an interview schedule (a sequenced list of prepared beginning interview questions). It is important that students think seriously about what they want to know about the person and his or her life.

Once they have created the questions, students should find quotes and reference materials to answer each one. This, in turn, may lead to revising the questions. The product of this work then has to be crafted into a scripted interview. The students choose another individual from the class to perform the interview with them. Their partner does the part of the interviewer, and they themselves assume the role of the historical person.

This activity enables students to go beyond the superficial summary of history that appears in most textbooks. Students can develop a sense of being the expert on something. It also encourages weighing and selecting facts on the basis of importance and priority. Students are actively engaged in their own learning (NMSA, 2010). In addition, their own values are called to account, and they become better decision makers.

Conclusion

In this chapter, we have attempted to describe the importance of inquiry to teaching middle school social studies. We presented a description of the inquiry process and examined the components of inquiry. While inquiry may limit the range of content coverage, it increases the depth of coverage. This is a good trade. How students achieve this depth depends on the type of inquiry they utilize. A developed typology of different kinds of inquiry was the basis for the model activities that were shared in the chapter.

Inquiry has a symbiotic relationship with key components of AMLE's vision for the middle school. These elements include broadening students' interests, developing their independence and work habits as learners, and allowing them to clarify and incorporate their values into decision making. An inquiring spirit is absolutely essential for lifelong learners.

Additional Inquiry Activities

1. Students can examine paintings or photographs from a particular place and period of time and try to describe verbally the life and culture of the time and place depicted. For example, show students sketches from Leonardo Da Vinci's sketchbook and ask about the purposes of the items he has drawn? What do the drawings say about his interests? For photographs and paintings, we look for the evidences of the culture and settings of the subjects as well as those of the painter to complete document analysis questions.

2. Provide students with the transcripts or summaries of crucial court cases. Students then write their predictions with the outcomes of the case and compare them to the actual outcomes. The teacher may use Famous Trials, *http://law2.umkc.edu/faculty/projects/ftrials/ftrials.htm*, for this activity to look at the significance of issues discussed in these cases.

3. Describe key historical events, and let students in groups discuss these descriptions, researching the historical context in order to make logical hypotheses related to the multiple factors causing the events. For example, the Zimmerman Telegraph activity discussed in chapter eight allows students to examine why Mexico refused to agree to this offer.

4. Have students research and make educated guesses about the reasons for the location and growth of particular cities like Atlanta and New Orleans throughout the 20th and 21st century. Students will look for factors such as resources, transportation, and population movement.

5. Have students discuss and research the question, "Why do we need constitutions for the individual states?" They might first want to examine the need for a national constitution. Students may then explore why the existence of a national constitution warrants the need for state constitutions.

References

Dewey, J. (1910). *How we think.* Boston, MA: D.C. Heath & Co.

Engle, S. (1960). Decision making: The heart of the social studies. *Social Education, 24*(7), 301-306.

Evans, R. (2004). *The social studies wars.* New York, NY: Teachers College Press.

Fiensterwal, J. (2015). *A great awakening for history and social studies.* Retrieved from http://edsource.org/2015/a-great-awakening-for-history-and-social-studies/77748.

Martin-Hansen, L. (2002). Defining inquiry. *Science Teacher, 69*(2), 34-37.

NMSA. (2010). *This we believe: Keys to educating young adolescents.* Westerville, OH: Author.

NCSS. (2013). *The college, career, and civic life (C3) framework for social studies state standards: Guidance for enhancing the rigor of K-12 civics, economics, geography, and history.* Retrieved from http://socialstudies.org/c3.

NCSS. (2016). A vision of powerful teaching and learning in social studies. *Social Education, 80*(3), 180-182.

Quillen, I. (2013).*Why inquiry learning is worth the trouble.* Retrieved from http://ww2.kqed.org/mindshift/2013/01/29/what-does-it-take-to-fully-embrace-inquiry-learning.

Ravitch, D. (2015). *Coaches shouldn't teach history.* George Mason University: History News Network. Retrieved from http://historynewsnetwork.org/article/1417.

Stephenson, N. (2007). *An introduction to inquiry based learning.* Retrieved from http://www.teachinquiry.com/index/Introduction.html.

Washington, E. & Dahlgren, R. (2010). "The quest for relevancy." Allan Kownslar and historical inquiry in the New Social Studies Movement. In. B. Stern (Ed.), *The new social studies: People, projects, and perspectives* (95-110). Charlotte, NC: Information Age Publishing.

03

Discussion in the Beehive of the Middle School Classroom

Discussion is human nature and middle school mania. It is also a strategy that has the potential to be one of the best uses of teaching time or one of the worst. The reasons are complicated, but then the art of doing discussion is not simple either. Discussion can be wild and wooly, or it can be dull and boring. When discussion works, it can open middle school students' minds and help them become better problem solvers (Halvorsen, 2012).

The purpose of this chapter is to help middle school teachers learn about using different types of discussion purposefully, preparing for and conducting discussions better, and sharing some model activities of discussion. In the process, we want to share some secrets to keeping discussions lively. We also want to do some problem solving to help teachers avoid the pitfalls and difficulties of setting up and leading good discussions. Different types of discussions are modeled with example activities. Our framing of discussion connects to AMLE's *This We Believe* (NMSA, 2010).

Car Chases, Blowing Up Stuff, and Amazing Races: Making Great Discussions Happen

The ultimate goal of classroom discussion is meaningful participation. We want to have all students be mentally and verbally involved. For that to seem remotely possible, teachers need to plan their discussions thoroughly and be absolutely inspired in how they motivate students to participate (Power & Power, 2013).

The problem with motivation is that it needs to come from inside the individual. Students do not take part in discussion because they do not understand or see the relevance of the material, or because cultural and peer values inhibit participation (Eberly Center, 2015).

The National Council for the Social Studies (NCSS) stresses that the most essential pre-requisite for student participation is to create a safe and accepting atmosphere in the classroom (NCSS, 1991). Students need to feel that whatever they say will be valued, not laughed at, derided, or criticized.

The definitive ways to inspire student motivation include mind-catching problems or questions (NCSS, 2016). This means adding a little suspense or mystery to the structure of the discussion. Teachers also need to realize that students participate for different reasons. Students need to be motivated in different ways to get them to participate. For example, if students are role-playing and are caught up in their roles, they instantly become bigger stakeholders in the outcome of the discussion itself.

Problem-based discussions can inspire middle schoolers' curiosity. Still another way to capture the Indiana Jones in all middle schoolers is to present them with scenarios that end in cliffhangers. These scenarios grab their attention and contain a role-playing element that allows them to participate in various leadership roles (Barton & Levstik, 2004). For example, when each student possesses a unique piece of information that no other student has, nothing can stop him or her from finding a way to make it count.

Finally, students' participation involves focusing their attention on asking—not just answering—questions. The best discussions evolve into patterns where students are in an exchange of ideas (Levstik & Barton, 2015). Once students ask good questions, they are genuinely curious and ultimately involved. Coming up with good questions is therefore in itself an important skill. The ability to phrase questions well reflects a thorough understanding of what the learner does and does not know.

Teaching Questioning Skills to Middle School Students

Good student questions reflect involved minds. This shows that students are curious about issues and ideas being discussed. Such questions have several defining qualities. They are clearly stated, focused, and purposeful. They show real curiosity, especially when students learn to ask open-ended questions. While they are sometimes provoked by previous discussions, they are more often well thought out over time. First and foremost, though, good questions are provocative of further discussion (Skills You Need, 2015).

One of the essentials in teaching questioning skills is to help students realize the importance of questioning words. One group of these is often referred to as the "5 W's" – Who, What, When, Where, and Why. Each of these words suggests a particular kind of answer. They break down and identify a separate component of the phenomenon they are describing or attempting to tell. These "5 W's", along with one other question word "how," can be combined to progressively explore an issue or problem thoroughly. Answers to the "5W's" questions create a more complete picture of any event.

There are other trade secrets in questioning. Teachers may help students understand how to restate questions through the Socratic method. The Socratic method involves learning and realizing that there are different types of questions with different purposes (Intel Teach Program, 2007). These include clarification questions, information and consequence questions, and viewpoint questions. Each of these kinds of questions helps the questioner to better understand what he or she already knows. Either through explanation, elaboration, or source identification, the questioner is better informed about issues by answering them.

Discussions Done Right

Teachers need to realize that purposeful discussions take planning. Hale and City (2006, p. 24) emphasize developing a "culture of inquiry." Obviously, the teacher needs to pre-think the key questions and prods to get students going (Edutopia, 2013). Teachers also should develop at the very least the following skills:

- Clearly communicating and selling the purpose of the discussion.
- Setting up deterrents to students sniping at and making fun of contributions.
- Getting students to listen to one another.
- Helping students develop ownership and control of discussions.
- Making students feel good about their contributions.
- Keeping the discussion going and on pace.

Discussions are on the clock. Appropriate amounts of time need to be allowed to develop the discussion together. During that time, we want to bring meaning to the entire discussion and set up how the discussion applies to the next activity. There are several ways for a teacher to close a discussion. We will suggest only three:

1. Lead or get students to lead a short summarization of the discussion.

2. Re-direct the discussion to talk about how it relates to an assessment, project, or activity.

3. Pose an exit question for them to answer as they leave the classroom.

Well-conducted discussions help students process knowledge, reinforce learned information, and give meaning to isolated bits of learning.

Different Kinds of Discussions

Discussions take different forms because they serve different purposes. The teacher always has to set the time and purpose (Hess, 2009). She has the additional constant role of controlling the pace and direction of the discussion. Some discussions would die without the teacher injecting new questions and comments. Others would bog down like a group of campers lost in a swamp if the teacher did not lead the students out of the quagmire.

We offer six different types of discussion in Figure 3.1. Each type serves a different teaching purpose and requires different types of thinking on the part of both the teacher and students. All six connect to AMLE's *This We Believe*. Such discussions are mostly teacher directed and teacher led, but they work better if the students ask intelligent, useful questions to help the teacher know what to clarify.

Figure 3.1 *Types of Discussions*

Type of Discussion	Purpose	Teacher/Student Roles and Participation
Explanatory	To provide clear description of an assignment or project or to give an overview of a course of study.	Teacher leads with provision of necessary description information.

Figure 3.1 (continued) *Types of Discussions*

Planning	To organize and delegate responsibility related to the successful accomplishment of a project or activity.	The teacher sets the agenda and clarifies questions and ideas, helps find consensus, and keeps the planning going.
Viewpoint/ Perspective	To learn to identify possible viewpoints about a topic or topics and to compare and contrast them.	The teacher provides catalysts and stimuli as well as clarifying the conflicts while keeping the peace.
Issues Exploration	To identify and look at the importance and relevance of all elements and perspectives related to issues.	The teacher guides the discussion and asks exploratory and clarifying questions.
Problem Solving	To develop skill in problem identification and clarification, to evaluate what is evidence, and weigh how information fits together and relates to a question or problem.	The teacher is guide.
Review/ Recap	To reinforce and pull together information previously studied; to sum up and give cohesion to an entire topic.	The teacher assures that all information and ideas that are important are covered, keeps the pace, and assures wide participation.

In order to understand the differences among these archetypes, a brief explanation of each needs to be explored. We provide these in the next sections. The explanations are accompanied by examples of discussion activities.

Explanatory Discussion

Explanatory discussions generally are used early in any social studies units. They may be used to prepare students for a reading or as formative evaluation. This type of discussion requires teachers to really work to get students to ask questions. The example offered is an exploration of the importance and impact of speeches made by public figures.

Great Speeches of History: Teacher Discussion Possible Script

Today you are going to analyze some great speeches. Yes, I know that it really sounds boring, but it is really going to be fun. We are going to look at the speeches in a way that you have never done before, and from these speeches, we are going to create a poem.

Teacher Introduction: What is a speech? Encourage students to give their own ideas. Try to bring out different definitions.

Follow Up Questions:

- Who gives speeches? (Encourage a wide scope of answers including: parents, teachers, principals, politicians, and ministers and priests.)

- I get the impression that most of you do not enjoy speeches. Why is that?

- If there are so many people who hate speeches, why do people give them? (Try to get students to think of several reasons including giving information, sharing dreams and ideas, and convincing people to do something.)

- Have you ever listened to a speech that really caught your attention, or one that made you laugh or cry? What was it about a speech that made you angry or inspired you? Have you ever heard a speech that was delivered so well, so dramatically, that it made you believe in what the speaker was saying? Those kinds of speeches were great speeches. If you have time, play Sojourner Truth's "Ain't I a Woman!" *(https://www.youtube. com/watch?v=XilHJc9IZvE)*. Other great speeches include Martin

Luther King, Jr.'s "I Have a Dream" speech *(https://www.youtube.com/ watch?v=3vDWWy4CMhE)* and Lincoln's Gettysburg address *(https://www. youtube.com/watch?v=_Dlggkx6mks).*

Now tell me, what are the qualities that make a speech great? Seek answers that suggest the passion and expression of the person speaking, the elegance of the words and their meaningfulness, and the power of the emotions that the speech stirs.

Well, we are going to look at some of those great speeches today. However, we are going to look at them in a very different way. First of all, let me give you the really good news: all of the speeches that we are using are very short. Here is the bad news; you are going to have to read them very carefully. There is even more good news. Although we are examining a lot of speeches, each of you is going to only look at one speech.

First of all, I am going to divide you into groups of four. Each group will have copies of a different speech. Everyone will need a highlighter, a felt tip marker, and four strips of paper.

Now, I am going to give you four steps to follow in exact order. Put these on a slide. Do not do anything until you know all of the steps.

Step 1: When I tell you to, take your highlighter as you read through the speech and highlight all of the phrases that you think are powerful and strong. Hopefully, there will be at least 8 or 10 different phrases or even whole sentences where you like the words, the emotion, or the idea.

Step 2: I then want you to identify your four favorites among these highlighted phrases and copy each of them LENGTHWISE on a different strip of paper.

Step 3: The third step is for the group to get together and take all of these strips of paper to construct a poem. Now this poem will be what we call "free verse" because it will not rhyme. However, it will have what we call "flow," that is, it will have a single message.

Now, someone is going to ask me about lines that repeat. Among your 16 or more lines, you may have some lines that repeat. What that means is that more than one person liked them. This is okay. If a line appears four times, then use it four times.

Step 4: Rewrite the whole poem on one piece of paper and then prepare to give it orally to the rest of the class. Tomorrow you can illustrate your poem. Follow up with reading and discussing the poems. Here are a few Internet sources to find speech texts: American Rhetoric Top 100 Speeches (http://www.americanrhetoric. com/top100speechesall.html), The 35 Greatest Speeches in History *(http://www. artofmanliness.com/2008/08/01/the-35-greatest-speeches-in-history)*, and Great American Speeches *(http://www.greatamericandocuments.com/speeches)*.

Examining the great speeches of history not only helps students to realize the impact of effective speechmaking but helps them look at the components of persuasive language. It enables students to better comprehend the greatness of particular figures in history (Austin & Thompson, 2015). In *This We Believe*, AMLE advocates "They (students) deserve opportunities to ascertain their special interests and aptitudes, to engage in activities that will broaden their views of the world and of themselves" (NMSA, 2010, p. 20). Studying the great speeches of the world can even lead middle school students to greatness themselves.

Planning Discussion: Ancient "Greek Walmart"

Planning discussions are used to launch projects and assignments. They involve both defining and explaining by the teacher as well as a give and take of clarifying questions and comments by both the teacher and the students. Teachers have to deal with the fact that students do not want to sound foolish. Therefore, they have to provoke comments and questions (Hess, 2004).

The concept of optimal fuzziness has to be part of the teacher's arsenal. The teacher wants to get enough specificity into the directions for the students to "get" what they are to do, yet not set the parameters to such specificity that everyone produces exactly the same thing. Planning discussions accomplish such tasks as delegating roles and jobs in group projects and stimulating creativity. The next section describes the discussion activity in itself.

Teacher Introduction: Where does your family do most of its shopping? Discuss their contributions and make a list.

Most of the students will agree that Walmart is one of the chains where a lot of people shop. Where did the ancient Greeks shop? Introduce the word "agora." Talk about how the agora compared to shopping centers. Brainstorm a list of products (see Figure 3.2) that might be sold in an agora, or if they prefer to call it a "Greek Walmart."

Figure 3.2 *Items that Might be Sold*

Sandals	Weapons	Olives and Olive Oil	Poultry	Dyes
Tunics	Farm Tools	Vegetables	Cows, Goats, and Sheep	Bread and Pastry
Fabrics	Shop Tools	Fruits such as Grapes, Figs, and Dates	Horses and Donkeys	Milk and other Drinks
Money Changers/ Lenders	Utensils for Cooking and Eating	Spices and Salt	Musical Instruments	Ink and Parchment
Armor and Helmets	Ceramics and Pottery	Perfume and Make-Up	Jewelry	Statues

Plan and map with the students an agora for the classroom. Think about the location. Activities such as this discussion help students see similarities and differences between modern and ancient cultures (Giles, Wang, Smith, & Johnson, 2013). Such activities also develop brainstorming skills, which are important for problem solving. As stated in AMLE's *This We Believe* (2010), " Having students grapple with and master advanced concepts and skills requires middle grades teachers to stretch themselves, moving well beyond 'covering material'" (p. 18).

ACTIVITY

Viewpoint/Perspective Discussion: The Civil War Nurses

A third type of discussion looks at getting students to understand viewpoints and perspectives. This type of discussion may focus on perspectives that are not the ones that students share. They may often be in debate formats in which students advocate for particular points of view. For example, if students play the parts of Thomas Jefferson or James Madison on the subject of the U.S. Constitution, they can see different points of view. Believing that all Americans were united in their thinking creates a misleading stereotype. In the next section, we present a discussion related to an often ignored group during the U.S. Civil War: female nurses.

Teacher Introduction: Dorothea Dix (1802-1887) was one of the early social reformers in this country. She fought for reform in mental health facilities and in treatment of prisoners. In 1861 with the outbreak of the U.S. Civil War, Dorothea Dix offered her services to the Union Army. She argued strongly that women should serve as nurses. Up until then, only men had been nurses. Dorothea argued so strongly that she won her case, and the Secretary of War appointed her Superintendent of Army Nurses.

Transition: Talk about Dorothea Dix's lack of qualifications (she was not a nurse and had no medical training). However, she did have very definite ideas on what kind of women should be nurses. Show students Circular No. 8 by Dorothea Dix found online at *http://womenshistory.about.com/od/civilwarnursing/a/nurses_circular.htm*. The following section deals with focus questions on the qualifications for nurses.

Discussion Questions:

1. Look at the qualifications for female nurses that Ms. Dix imposed. What do you think of them?

2. What do you think that Dorothea Dix was trying to accomplish? What was she trying to prevent?

3. What groups of women are excluded by these qualifications? Why do you think they were excluded?

4. How are nurses trained today? Are nurses all women, or do you know some men? Tell us about them.

5. What makes people want to be nurses?

This discussion alerts students to the changing role of women in society during the U.S. Civil War. Such a discussion ties into what AMLE terms as the "hidden curriculum" through which students learn about stereotypes and gender roles (NMSA, 2010, p. 18). It may lead to further discussions of modern society and the degree to which modern views of women need to be changed. Students should be aware that gender roles are evolving and that this change causes conflict.

Issues Exploration Discussion: The Election of 1820

Discussions that explore issues take perspectives to a different level altogether. Such discussions are really for the purpose of "unpacking" particular issues. They begin with clear and complete defining and explaining of what the issues are and why they are "issues." The more students know and the stronger their opinions are about the issues, the more leadership they can take. The teacher's role can become more that of devil's advocate or, in some cases, peace keeper. Such conversations can become divisive if the teacher does not show wisdom and judgment. The objective is to help students see different sides of issues more clearly and to empathize with people that have different viewpoints than their own (Endacott & Brooks, 2013).

Teacher Introduction: Today, we are going back in history to the Election of 1820. I did not pick this year because it was a hard fought, controversial, close election. It was the very opposite. James Monroe was easily elected with his only opponent, John Quincy Adams, receiving only one electoral vote. This was called the "Era of Good Feelings." I picked this election because it was a period in which a lot of issues were taking shape that would influence the United States for the next 50 years. We are going to look at these issues as though we were backing a presidential candidate, writing speeches, and building a platform. Here are some of the issues of that period.

Expansion of the United States: Illinois and Alabama were new states participating in their first election.

Slavery: The Missouri Compromise had momentarily eased tension between Northern congressmen who wanted to ban slavery in all new states admitted to the Union and Southerners that wanted to preserve the institution of slavery.

The Economy: A depression had gripped the nation since 1815.

Expansion: Many people wanted more land opened up for settlement.

Tariffs: American manufacturers had gotten Congress to pass a large Protective Tariff in 1816. Southerners and Westerners wanted free trade to keep prices down.

Banking: The Second Bank of the United States was established in 1816 to stabilize currency. Many Westerners and Southerners opposed it.

Foreign Policy: There was concern over European powers continuing to hold colonies in Central and South America.

Teacher Directions: Political parties really were not an issue in 1820. It was a one-candidate race. For this activity, we will create two political parties. (Pass out red and blue stickers to denote the members of two political parties.) Now each of our parties does not have a candidate. What we want is a campaign platform for whatever candidate each party runs. I want each party to sit in a circle.

Either delegate or find a quick form of electing a discussion leader and a scribe for each party. Designate a pair of students to research each issue and report to the group. The research can be done online, or you can provide a hand out of information on each issue. Instruct the groups to spend a designated time researching the issues before reporting back to the group. Then, have the group come up with a policy statement on each category.

Part of the middle school philosophy as identified in *This We Believe* is that "An effective middle grades curriculum is distinguished by learning experiences that address societal expectations while appealing to young adolescents and offering them opportunities to pose and answer questions that are important to them" (NMSA, 2010, p. 17). This discussion activity embodies this concept by helping students to understand a lot about campaign issues and party platforms. Students will also learn that issues change with the times (Clabough, Turner, Russell, & Waters, 2016).

Problem Solving Discussion: Ancient Greek Myths and Stories

Problem solving discussions can be the most enjoyable and satisfying, but they can also be frustrating. Such discussions encourage student leadership and independence. Problem solving discussions are closely linked to inquiry and student research. Though it is an oversimplification, problem solving may involve problems of two types. The first type does have a knowable and verifiable correct answer. Questions such as "What were George Washington's views of developing alliances and relationships with other nations?" can be answered by looking at the first president's speeches and letters. The second type is more difficult. Many problems have no single, simple solution, or the solutions are based on values and emotions. It is also true that the situations themselves may change, and the problems are simply unsolvable.

Teacher Introduction: The heroes of Greek myths were always having to solve problems. They might be given trials to pass or challenged to make choices where anything they did was bound to bring some sort of trouble. What are some myths that you know? If they need hints mention Hercules, as well as Rick Riordan's books (2014; 2015). They may also know Peter Lerangis' *Seven Wonders Series* (2013).

Well one such Greek hero is just a man, and his name was Theseus. There are several myths about him, but the most famous is the story of the Minotaur. Does anyone know anything about this story?

Invite comments on the differences between gods and men to the Greeks. There are lots of versions of the Greek myths and especially of the Minotaur story. They include the following: *http://www.greekmyths-greekmythology.com/myth-of-theseus-and-minotaur, https://www.youtube.com/watch?v=lJV7mv_mX5c, http://*

www.mythweb.com/encyc/entries/theseus.html, and https://www.youtube.com/
watch?v=c5TK0PnXMz4.

We are going to look at only part of the myth. Then, I am going to ask you about the choices Theseus has and the decisions that he needs to make. We are going to look at three things: What are the problems he has to solve? What are his choices? What are the possible consequences of each choice?

Here is the backstory. Theseus is the young son of the King of Athens. A few years ago, Minos the King of Crete, sent his son to Athens to compete in the Panathenaic Games. A bull killed that son. This made King Minos very angry, so he threatened the city of Athens with a plague if they did not send seven young men and women to Crete every year. What the King did with these young people was terrible and frightening. Anyone want to guess what it was?

Minos had built this really huge and creepy labyrinth. He had built it years before as a prison for his stepson, who was this enormous half bull and half man called the Minotaur. Now, all that the Minotaur ate was human flesh. When the Athenian young people arrived, King Minos sent them down into the Labyrinth. They wandered through until the Minotaur caught them. (Line up seven boys and seven girls before you tell this last part.)

Now this went on for three years and on the third year, Theseus volunteered to go. Would you volunteer? All right, I want you to imagine you are Theseus entering the maze. What are your problems? Encourage discussion and ask probing questions. Students should be able to come up with several problems including:

1. How do you find your way through the Labyrinth?

2. How to fight the Minotaur and win?

3. How do you then get away from King Minos and the Cretans? (Remember that Crete is an island).

Talk about the kinds of labyrinths students have experienced. These may include Halloween Corn Mazes or Halls of Mirrors. Discuss the problems of taking on a huge fierce animal with the cunning of a man.

Now tell the students that you have left one little thing out. Somehow when Theseus first got to Crete, he met Ariadne, King Minos' daughter. Now she thought he was a rock star and fell madly in love with him at first sight. How does that change things for Theseus? How can Ariadne help her new boyfriend? Allow students to speculate about how Ariadne might help Theseus with each of his problems. Tell the rest of the story. Speculate about what happened to Ariadne with the students.

This kind of activity helps students to better understand that myths are how people record their past. Myths are the basis of historical pride and embody the values of a people. This knowledge helps students to understand the people themselves from their technology to their principles of right and wrong (Wineburg, Martin, & Monte-Sano, 2012). This type of discussion enables students to interact with the curriculum in challenging and integrative ways (NMSA, 2010).

 ## Review/Recap Discussion: American Revolution

The sixth type of discussion on our chart is referred to as the review or recap discussion. The major purpose is to review and summarize what students have learned about a time period. Students certainly can direct and lead such discussions, but the teacher's job is to make sure the conversation covers all that is important and useful. The review is important because it reinforces learning and helps make all the pieces covered a period of study fit together.

Teacher Introduction: Begin the discussion by drawing students to immediately take the lead. This may take several attempts. The series of questions may progress as follow. Open with a very broad "Can someone start us off?" If that is unproductive, move to the following questions.

- What about a timeline? Where should we start it? (Have a student put it on the board or add it to a PowerPoint) Now, we can start filling in the other events. Let us get them down. We can rearrange them later. (At the minimum events such as the Proclamation of 1763, the various tax acts, the Townsend Acts, the Quartering Act, and the Boston Tea Party as well as other battles need to be discussed and then ordered when reviewing the American Revolutionary War era.)

- By the time the Second Continental Congress got together in 1775, we can agree that things had really escalated. What did the American colonists want at that time? Look at the Declaration of Independence. Talk about Patrick Henry's "Give me Liberty" speech as well as Thomas Paine's *Common Sense.*

- What do you think brought the Congress to the point of no return? What is Thomas Jefferson really saying in the Declaration of Independence? What do you think was the impact of the Declaration of Independence in the American colonies and in Britain?

- Now let us talk about the war itself. Did things go well for the colonists— let's call them the Continental Army—all along?

- Why did things begin to change, and how did they change? How did the Continental Army itself change? What were the contributions of sympathizers including Baron Von Steuben and the Marquis de Lafayette? Talk about the changing tide of war with growing number of victories including those at Trenton and later Saratoga.

- You all know about Mt. Rushmore and the four presidents whose faces were carved there. If you were to build a "Mt. Rushmore" just representing the American Revolution, whose faces do you think should be depicted on it and why?

This kind of discussion allows the teacher to prepare students for any evaluation. "As they develop the ability to hypothesize, organize information into useful and meaningful constructs, and grasp long-term cause and effect relationships, students demonstrate they are ready for and should play a major role in their own education" (NMSA, 2010, p. 16). It helps students to see the important events of the American Revolution and their significance. This approach to discussion can be easily adapted to any historical time period.

Making Class Discussions Work

The type of the discussion is one of the determinants of how long it will last. Of course, the optimum length of a discussion is a function of a number of factors. These include the purpose and type of discussion, the time available, and the level of student participation and interest.

For discussion to work, most of the students need to want to participate and have the opportunity to do so (Halvorsen, 2012). We want them to be both mentally and verbally engaged. We even want students to take charge. However, guiding the discussion so that this occurs in a meaningful way is not easy. Additionally, teachers can never let the train of discussion run off the tracks. They have to listen to every word and be constantly alert for problems and the need to redirect and refocus.

Teachers have to clearly and insightfully guide. Hale and City (2006, p. 10) suggest that teachers need to be "architects" of discussions, providing and communicating the plan. They sometimes have to step in to nudge and encourage students to follow up, particularly when important points are made. Teacher concerns include the following:

- Initiating and provoking the discussion.
- Keeping the discussion focused.

- Pacing the discussion.

- Keeping the pulse and tone of the discussion at acceptable levels.

- Emphasizing and elaborating on key points.

- Bringing the discussion to a close.

Middle school students like to talk. Discussion should be easy; it is not. Discussion can be an easily abused and misused teaching tool. However, when it does work, it is a super-tool. Students get excited about topics and issues. They take ownership of their own learning, and they become independent learners (Power & Power, 2013). "Such activities foster student ownership and lead to levels of understanding unlikely to be achieved when students are simply completing teacher-made assignments" (NMSA, 2010, p. 16). The teacher is the queen bee and the classroom becomes a beehive where every bee knows its job and does it.

Additional Discussion Activities

1. Discuss ideas you "hate." There are many ideas and practices which have been popular in the world that students dislike and even hate. Start a discussion about what was appealing to people at the time that made these practices and ideologies even possible. How could people ever be led to accept them? Examples would include: slavery, the Holocaust, genocide, the use of terrorist strategies (Remind them of the Swamp Fox, Francis Marion during the American Revolution), the beheading of Charles I, and capital punishment.

2. It is all in the details. Have students examine maps, paintings, and/or photographs and point out details and factors that give them more meaning. For example, in Raphael's painting of St. George and the dragon, we might look at the style of the armor, the proportions of the horse, and the fashion style of the maiden. The interest should be on finding things not noticed at first glance or things that should not be there.

3. Present a scenario to the class and have them discuss it. An example of a scenario: It is the summer of 1778 in upstate New York. Your family has been farming the land here for three years. You know that the British have allied themselves with the Iroquois and that some farms have been attacked. Everyone works in the fields with a musket close by in case of trouble. One day you are working in a field. You spy four Iroquois moving across your farm toward your cabin. You are pretty sure that they have not seen you among the tall rows of corn. You grab your musket and powder horn and dive behind a nearby rock. As the Iroquois move toward your cabin, you realize that if you do not do something that your wife and children are likely to be taken by surprise and killed. However, if you fire a shot, your own position will be exposed. What do you do? More important, why do you do it?

4. You are casting a fictional historical movie for a major motion picture studio based on the American Revolution. What events do you portray? Who are the major historical characters? Who do you cast in those roles, and why do you choose them? This activity should help students look deeper into the personalities of historical figures.

5. Discuss summaries of crucial court cases and predict the verdicts of the Supreme Court. Important cases can be found at *http://www.streetlaw. org/en/landmark/home*. Such cases determine whether and how laws are enforced. The teacher can then discuss how students' rights are connected to these famous cases.

References

Austin, H. & Thompson, K. (2015). *Examining the evidence: Seven strategies for teaching with primary sources.* North Mankato, MN: Maupin House Publishing.

Barton, K. C., & Levstik, L. S. (2004). *Teaching history for the common good.* Mahwah, NJ: Lawrence Erlbaum.

Clabough, J., Turner, T., Russell, W., & Waters, S. (2016). *Unpuzzling history with primary sources.* Charlotte, NC: Information Age Publishing.

Eberly Center: Teaching Excellence and Educational Excellence and Innovation. Carnegie Mellon. (2015). *Solving a teaching problem. Students don't participate in discussion.* Retrieved from https://www.cmu.edu/teaching/solveproblem/strat-dontparticipate/index.html.

Edutopia (2013). *Beyond Q + A: Six strategies that motivate all students to participate.* Retrieved from http://www.edutopia.org/blog/6-strategies-motivate-student-participation-maddie-witter.

Endacott, J. & Brooks, S. (2013). An update theoretical and practical model for promoting historical empathy. *Social Studies Research and Practice, 8*(1), 41-57.

Giles, C., Wang, Y., Smith, J., & D. Johnson. (2013). "I'm no longer just teaching history." Professional development for teaching Common Core State Standards for literacy in social studies. *Middle School Journal, 44*(3), 34-42.

Hale, M. & City, E. (2006). *Leading student centered discussions.* Thousand Oaks, CA: Corwin Press.

Halvorsen, A. (2012). Facilitating discussions in social studies classrooms. In W. Russell III (Ed.), *Contemporary social studies: An essential reader* (385-398). Charlotte, NC: Information Age Publishing.

Hess, D. (2004). Discussion in social studies: Is it worth the trouble? *Social Education, 68*(2), 151-156.

Hess, D. (2009). *Controversy in the classroom: The democratic power of discussion.* New York, NY: Routledge.

Intel Teach Program: Designing Effective Projects. (2007). *The Socratic questioning technique.* Retrieved from http://www.intel.com/content/dam/www/program/education/us/en/documents/project-design/strategies/dep-question-socratic.pdf.

Lerangis, P. (2013). *Seven wonders book 1: The Colossus rises*. New York, NY: Harper Collins.

Levstik, L. & Barton, K. (2015). *Doing history: Investigating with elementary and middle schools* (5th ed.), New York, NY: Routledge.

NMSA. (2010). *This we believe: Keys to educating young adolescents*. Westerville, OH: Author.

NCSS. (1991). *Social studies in the middle school*. Retrieved from http://www.socialstudies. org/positions/middleschool.

NCSS. (2016). A vision of powerful teaching and learning in social studies. *Social Education, 80*(3), 180-182.

Power, C. & Power, A. (2013). From self-isolation to peer interaction: Building community in middle grades classrooms. In. K. Rooney & R. Lipka (Eds.), *Middle Grades Curriculum: Voices and visions of the self-enhancing school* (71-88). Charlotte, NC: Information Age Publishing.

Riordan, R. (2014). *Percy Jackson's Greek Gods*. New York, NY: Disney-Hyperion

Riordan, R. (2015). *Magnus Chase and the Gods of Asgard, book 1: The sword of summer.* New York, NY: Disney-Hyperion.

Skills You Need. (2011). Types of questions. Retrieved from http://www.skillsyouneed.com/ ips/question-types.html.

Wineburg, S., Martin, D., & Monte-Sano, C. (2012). *Reading like a historian: Teaching literacy in middle and high school history classrooms*. New York, NY: Teachers College Press.

04

Working with a Diverse Student Population

U.S. classrooms are becoming increasingly diverse. White students no longer make up half of the public school students. This changing landscape is expected to continue (Kena et al, 2014). Our schools have students with IEPs, those for whom English is a second language, students identified as gifted and talented, and students from minority groups. An AMLE (2010) essential attribute is to provide an equitable education that advocates and provides a challenging curriculum for all students. Unfortunately, in the latest National Assessment of Educational Progress (NAEP) history, civics, and geography scores of U.S. eighth graders, the achievement gap between white and minority groups remained wide and steady (NAEP, 2015). One reason for these results may be connected to teachers' classroom strategies frequently employed. For example, research has shown that social studies standards, texts, and instruction have frequently been cited as lacking diverse voices while being centered on Eurocentric perspectives (Loewen, 2008; Fitchett & Heafner, 2012). When certain narratives are more dominant than others, this can have a powerful negative influence on children's sense of identity and citizenship

(Peck, 2010). Research also suggests students are best served by a social studies classroom where multiple narratives co-exist (Barton & Levstik, 2004; Todd, 2011).

This chapter addresses these changing demographics in U.S. schools by examining how to structure the classroom and design activities to meet the learning needs of diverse modern middle schools. The concept of diversity is broad and can denote a variety of differences. Ethnic, cultural, and linguistic differences are often discussed areas within diversity and will be addressed. In this chapter, we also explore strategies for students with varying learning styles, interests, and diverse learning levels (e.g., gifted and talented). We give a variety of learning strategy examples that connect to AMLE's *This We Believe* (2010). An appendix with suggested resources is also provided.

Embracing Diversity

Zine (2002) notes that schools often attempt to recognize non-dominant cultures through events such as multicultural fairs or heritage months. Oftentimes, the result is that these events further lead to misconceptions and stereotypes while failing to explore the cultures' rich experiences. While usually subconscious, teachers often bring in their personal views of non-dominant cultures during instruction. Todd (2011) stated that in classrooms "cultural diversity is frequently synonymous with a view of individuals as the aggregate of their cultural attributes, a fact that prevents… adequate engagement with the very terms of conflict such educational endeavors seek to surmount" (p. 102). This further marginalizes these groups' voices.

Banks (2004) says that teacher dispositions and behaviors are essential for student success when working with diverse populations. Belknap and Hess (2000) identified the following common beliefs that some teachers bring into the classroom when focusing on diversity.

- Denying skin color as relevant.

- Belief that addressing diversity allows students to adopt a victim mentality.

- Lowered expectations of students from certain groups.

- Belief that within-group discrimination does not count.

- Paying lip service to diversity yet maintaining prejudice in words and actions.

- Using fear of the unknown as a protective cover.

This conception of diversity implies it to be something that needs to be managed rather than being a lived state, which risks further dehumanizing an individual and cultural group. To counter this, Ukpokodu (2003) identifies four factors teachers should consider to increase personal awareness of diversity issues while attempting to adapt the classroom to meet all students' needs.

- Become cognizant of the diversity among students in the classroom.

- Suspend habitual notions that presume sameness.

- Reexamine longstanding beliefs and assumptions about diverse learners.

- Strive to create classrooms where each student can succeed in different ways.

Implementation of appropriate multicultural instruction requires teacher acknowledgement and tolerance of the cultural diversity within our society. Employing a standardized instruction approach contradicts the nature of cultural plurality. Instructional best practices must allow students to explore cultural complexities and recognize that diversity exists in the interpretations of a social studies topic. Social studies should be helping students understand the processes for discussing societal challenges that they will encounter. Student-centered, authentic learning opportunities enable students to gain the skills necessary to do this by allowing them to express, interact, and share. The next few sections address a selection of diverse student populations and provide teaching recommendations for each group.

Multicultural Groups

Students' perceptions of social studies are greatly influenced by their individual perceptions (Jaffee, 2016); therefore, if students are to have impactful learning experiences, teachers must gain an understanding of students' cultural backgrounds in order to provide curricula relatable to the students. Unfortunately, U.S. education has not been very culturally responsive to ethnic and gender diversity, placing these groups at an academic disadvantage (Gay, 2002; Woyshner, 2012).

When developing multicultural lessons, teachers typically use either a single-group or multiple-perspectives focus. In a single-group approach, the students look at a cultural group in depth. It is important that this approach avoid stereotypes and distortions. The goal of this approach is typically to learn more about specific perspectives that students may be unfamiliar with connected to a cultural group. Teachers should be going beyond the surface level introduction of such items as a group's clothing, food, or religious preferences. Instead, there should be careful analysis of values, ethics, and core beliefs.

In a multiple-perspectives approach, the curriculum focuses on a single issue and analyzes how it is viewed by several groups. This approach helps students recognize the varied ways different groups interpret events.

Etlin (1988) provides a checklist that teachers can consider while assessing multicultural resources for classroom use.

1. Does the text or other instructional material give proportionate coverage to our country's different ethnic groups?

2. Does it present them in the variety of roles and situations that all our country's people deal with rather than limit them to one or two stereotypical contexts?

3. Does it present stories and historical incidents from the point of view of the people concerned, whatever their ethnic group, rather than that of the traditional single-culture U.S. society?

4. Does it use language that recognizes the dignity of the groups involved, not using demeaning slang terms? Does it avoid using dialect unless it is presented respectfully and serves a necessary purpose?

5. If it is fiction, does the storyline avoid distributing power and competence on the basis of ethnic group stereotypes?

Gender Issues

Studies consistently show children prefer same gender protagonists (Chick & Heilman-Houser, 2000; McCabe, Fairchild, Grauerholz, Pescosolido, & Tope, 2011). Unfortunately, female voices have largely been absent from social studies textbooks and classrooms (Scheiner-Fisher & Russell, 2012). Recently, online collections of primary sources related to women's history, as well as primary source document books marketed to history and social studies instructors, have increased (Libressco & Balantic, 2013). This increased access to primary sources provides opportunities for females to receive a significant role in the curriculum. When teaching about gender issues, recommendations for teachers include the following.

- Be attentive to details or clues that indicate stereotyping, bias, distortion, or omission of key issues in materials dealing with gender. For example, students can analyze and discuss textbook bias, treatment of women, and famous women who have been omitted.

- Provide students with examples of females who occupy a variety of responsible roles.

- In order to contrast sources, use firsthand accounts of females when possible.

- Have gender issues lessons that include both "insider" and "outsider" accounts, primary and secondary sources so that students have a variety of views from which to analyze and draw conclusions.

- Incorporate outside resources (e.g., community members and organizational leaders) to provide students with real-life female representatives.

- Make women's history inclusive and interesting for all students. This can be done by incorporating hands-on, student-centered activities that allow students to challenge stereotypes and explore their interests.

These recommendations can personalize and make relevant the curriculum for all students.

English Language Learners

The amount of English Language Learners (ELL) in public schools in the 2012-2013 school year was approximately four and a half million or 9.2% (U.S. Department of Education, 2015). Further, the number of ELLs increased in 39 states from 2002 to 2013 (U.S. Department of Education, 2015). Typically, ELLs are mainstreamed into regular classrooms (Cruz & Thornton, 2008). One of the major challenges social studies teachers face involves adjusting content and instruction to meet the needs of this increasing ELL population. Research has suggested teachers need to provide linguistically and culturally responsive instruction for ELLs in social studies courses that take into consideration the students' social, cultural, political, and economic contexts in the United States (Yoder, Kibler, & van Hover, 2016; Jaffee, 2016).

Linguistically, it is important that instructors have a cursory understanding of language development. According to the "Natural Approach," there are four levels of language development: Pre-Production, Early Production, Speech Emergence, and Intermediate Fluency (Krashen & Terrell, 1983). The Pre-Production stage is often found among ELL students who have recently arrived in the United States. In the Early Production stage, students are beginning to develop basic interpersonal communication skills. During Speech Emergence, they start to feel more comfortable with the language and begin to attempt sentences and participate in conversations. The Intermediate Fluency stage often takes three to four years of English language immersion. At this point, students engage in everyday conversations with ease but are often reluctant to speak in front of large groups.

Language difficulties represent just one difficulty for ELL students. These students also commonly encounter difficulties with differing cultural mores and backgrounds, a lack of background knowledge, an inability to connect with the ways teachers organize the social studies content, and difficulty with the cultural concepts used to introduce some of the social studies content. For these reasons, culturally responsive instruction is critical. Figure 4.1 provides strategies that can be used with ELL social studies students specific to each language stage, which was adapted from Cruz and Thornton (2008).

Figure 4.1 *ELL Speech Stages & Strategies*

Stage	When	Example Activities
PreProduction	Recently arrived in U.S.	Use contexualized language (e.g., gestures, realia, picture for context clues, word banks, and word walls).
Early Production	About one year into U.S. schooling.	Patterned language usage and the use of contextual language is critical. Use of context clues is effective. Graphic organizers and story maps are helpful for students during this stage. Use questions that list words, require Yes/No or Either/Or.
Speech Emergence	Typically, after one to three years of English exposure.	Teacher models reading strategies (e.g., use features such as chapter overviews and bolded vocabulary words). Participate in group writing activities and reading literature they select themselves. Provide opportunities for these students to use English in a variety of contexts.
Intermediate Fluency	Approximately three to four years after arriving in U.S.	Can read academic texts, do journal writing, oral reports, and storytelling. Provide role-playing opportunities.

This table can help teachers navigate the different stages of ELL students' language development.

Gifted and Talented

Gifted and talented students display outstanding abilities, talents, or skills in one or more diverse manners. They may be high intellectual achievers or show an extraordinary talent in a single field, such as science, math, or art. It is estimated that up to 40% of identified gifted students are at risk of failing or performing far below their potential (Seeley, 2004) and reversal of underachievement by gifted students continues to be largely unresolved (Rayneri, Gerber, & Wiley, 2006). School curricula that are dull and unchallenging do not encourage gifted students to develop necessary skills (Diaz, 1998). It takes challenging and engaging curriculum to motivate them (Kaplan, 1990). Without motivation, gifted students may continue to exhibit mild to severe underachievement (Davis & Rimm, 1998).

The two most common methods for working with this population is through acceleration and enrichment programs. Acceleration programs allow students to go through existing school programs at a quicker pace. Examples include grade skipping, subject acceleration, in which the student goes to a higher grade for a specific subject, and telescoping, where students may complete two academic years in one (Bailey, 2004). Enrichment programs keep gifted and talented students with their age group, but they receive more sophisticated and demanding instruction than others in the classroom. It is important to note that enrichment activities are not those that would be considered busy work and add extra class or homework that are more of the same or an end in itself. Enrichment needs to give students choices and challenge them to go deeper in their thinking and analytical skills. It should be purposeful, focused, and planned. An example is having students who have been studying the Age of Exploration create an online virtual museum documenting this era.

Maker (1987) has suggested a number of research-based pedagogical techniques effective with gifted and talented students, such as the following.

- Assignments that challenge and pique curiosity
  (e.g., research projects and surveys)

- Using music, film, and art in a manner that improves analytical skills.

- Using controversial issues that juxtapose primary and secondary
  sources and conflicting accounts.

Student-centered activities that require active participation
(e.g., debates and simulations).

- Outside resources (e.g., experts and field trips).

- Depth (emphasizing critical thinking) over breadth.

- Using technology for research and simulation activities.

These strategies can be especially helpful for enrichment needs for gifted
and talented.

Students with Disabilities

The passage of the Individuals with Disabilities Education Act Amendments in
1997 and 2004 required that students with disabilities have access to the general
education curriculum. To meet the goal of equal access and enable each student
to engage with his or her lessons in a meaningful way, teachers must be prepared to
provide useful alternatives in terms of both curricular materials and instructional
delivery. Learning disability definitions are complex but include the following
key characteristics.

- Normal intelligence.

- Discrepancy between intelligence and classroom performance.

- Academic deficiencies in at least once subject.

- Lack of other disabilities such as mental retardation or behavioral disorders (Steele, 2007).

Students with disabilities, whether physical, emotional, or cognitive in nature, respond to the curriculum differently from their peers (Minarik & Lintner, 2016). For example, depending on the disability itself and other factors affecting their ability to succeed academically, they may need modifications such as advance and graphic organizers, instructional scaffolding, additional practice and time to complete assignments, and alternative media (e.g., large-print materials, audiotapes, or electronic materials). The standard curricular materials can be inadequate for these students without these specific modifications. Teachers need to adjust the materials or their presentation to break down the barriers and assist these students in learning.

Some common problem areas for students with learning disabilities include exhibiting reading and writing skills significantly below grade level (Steele, 2007). Processing and organizational deficits are also widespread deficits (Mercer & Mercer, 2005). It is also not uncommon for students with disabilities to have difficulty remembering information (Bos & Vaughn, 2006), which can lead to further difficulty in traditional teacher-centered social studies classrooms that rely on memorization.

A number of instructional adaptations have proved effective with students with disabilities. These adaptations include the following.

- Modify textbook instruction. For example, bring in historical fiction, graphic novels, and source materials that can be found on reliable Internet websites that may be easier for students to read (e.g., The Library of Congress and BBC).
- Provide modification and guidance for social studies writing. For example, model the construction of outlines, charts, and pre-writing strategies.

- Instruct students on directions and vocabulary typically used (e.g., explain, compare, analyze, and evaluate).

- Mnemonics are valuable for students who have difficulties remembering items. For example, students can use "grasp" to remember first amendment rights (freedom of grievance, religion, assembly, speech, and press).

- Emphasize organizational strategies, such as visual charts, webs, or timelines.

- Use activities that involve student engagement and relevance to students' lives. Examples may include simulations, role-plays, and group projects.

- Present smaller amounts of information; focus on one or two major points.

- Do demonstrations. Examples may include storytelling, speeches, show-and-tell projects, student-made bulletin boards, and songs.

- Provide frequent evaluation and feedback on incremental learning, with an emphasis on positive feedback.

These recommendations provide models for easy ways to differentiate learning for all students.

Diverse Learning Strategies

Culturally responsive teachers recognize and react to the changing cultural dynamics of the classroom. These culturally responsive teachers develop social studies curricula encouraging inquiry, perspective-taking, and higher-order thinking (Fitchet & Heafner, 2012). The following three activities demonstrate culturally-responsive diverse perspectives that can be incorporated into middle school social studies classrooms. Additionally, each activity uses strategies identified in the previous chapter sections' recommendations for the various diversity groups.

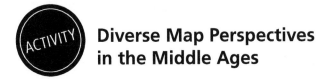

Diverse Map Perspectives in the Middle Ages

This is an introduction activity for a unit on the Middle Ages. The activity provides students a window into the thinking processes and perspectives of people from this time period that influenced travel, trade, and governance. It also demonstrates how diverse experiences influence our multiple perspectives of similar events and places.

To begin, students take out a sheet of paper and have seven minutes to draw a world map. Besides being told to draw the map, the only instructions students should be given are to avoid looking at maps around the room, not work with a partner, and include the most prominent points in the world. Afterwards, the students pair up and should answer the following questions:

1. How did your pictures differ?

2. How were they similar?

3. How accurate/inaccurate were your pictures?
   Elaborate on the reasons.

After about five minutes, the teacher leads a class discussion about these questions and points out how perceptions are different based on personal experiences. The teacher then shows students the upside down map (see Figure 4.2). Students look at perspectives that were prevalent during the Middle Ages by looking at some predominant maps during that period. A 4:30 minute video of "The Hereford Mappa Mundi" *(https://www.youtube.com/watch?v=uO-IJUP_UBQ)* is shown. Considered a detailed T-O map, it is the largest medieval map known to still exist. There are approximately 1,100 place-names, figurative drawings and inscriptions, and sources from biblical, classical, and Christian texts. During the short video, students should note the following:

- What do the visuals say about the people during this time?

- What helped influence places being identified (note: notice the comments about the Old Testament)?

Figure 4.2 *Upside Down Map*

Take the quiz! Compare country size. Which of the images on both sides of this placemat are "area accurate"? How is the Hobo-Dyer projection below different from the one on the reverse side? Answers and details about all the images are at *www.odt.irg/hdp*.
(1) Van ????? Geosphere,
(2) Gue??????? Toronto-centered projection,
(3) the Oxford Globe, and
(4) Goode's Ho???????????

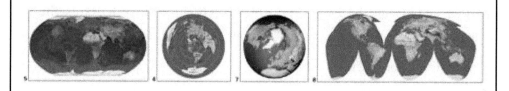

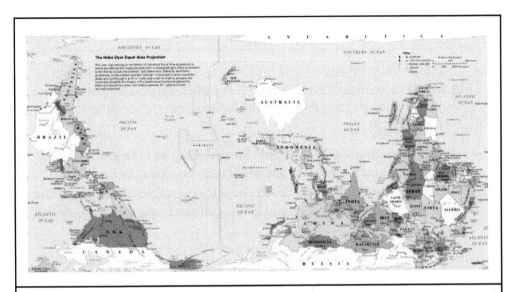

To order: ODT, Inc., ISBN 1-931057-11-7, 1-800-736-1293, Int'l Calls: 1-413-549-1293, *www.odt.org*, Email: odtstore@aol.com, Fax: 1-413-549-3503, Box 134, Amherst, MA 01004 USA

After the video, the teacher facilitates a class discussion around the two questions students were to be thinking about during the video viewing and then points out that geographers often look at the following three questions:

1. What is where?

2. Why there?

3. Why care?

Using these three geography questions, the teacher facilitates a discussion about the video. Next, the teacher introduces a series of maps from the Middle Ages that the students will look at in small groups. The following maps will be used (see Figure 4.3):

- "The T-O Map of Isidore of Seville"—(7th century) this map became the basis for many future medieval maps.

- "Beutus"—(8th century, around 776) Map based on the accounts given by Isidore of Seville, Ptolemy, and the Holy Bible. It includes placing the Garden of Eden at the end of Asia and locating a fourth continent beyond Africa.

- "Tabula Rogeriana"—(1154) Depicts Europe, Asia, and the northern part of Africa (the southern part of the world is at the top of the map). Al-Idrisi states that it shows "the seven climatic regions, with their respective countries and districts, coasts and lands, gulfs and seas, watercourses and river mouths."

Figure 4.3 *Maps From the Middle Ages*

The T-O Map of Isidore of Seville (7th century) this map became the basis for many future medieval maps

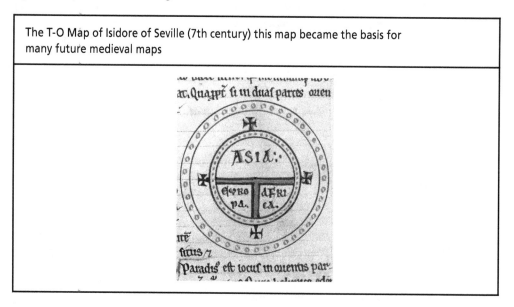

Beutus (8th century, around 776) Map based on the accounts given by Isidore of Seville, Ptolemy, and the Holy Bible. It includes placing the Garden of Eden at the end of Asia and locating a fourth continent beyond Africa.

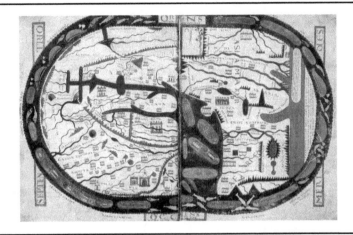

"Tabula Rogeriana" (1154) Depicts Europe, Asia, and the northern part of Africa (the southern part of the world is at the top of the map). Al-Idrisi states that it shows "the seven climatic regions, with their respective countries and districts, coasts and lands, gulfs and seas, watercourses and river mouths."

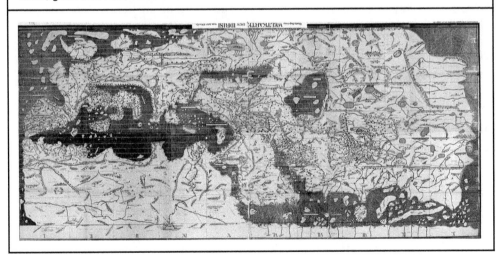

The teacher projects each map on the screen for a period of three to four minutes each, and the students work in their groups to answer the three geography questions about each map. Sticky notes should be provided to each group and the answers put on chart paper. It would be good to have nine chart papers around the room (three for each map). Below we have provided three questions for students to answer with each of these maps.

1. What is where (while answering this students should notice what is portrayed where it is portrayed on the map)?

2. Why there (students should be asked to speculate about why the cartographer may have placed things in the specific locations)?

3. Why care (students should provide answers as to what the repercussions for society during that time might be as a result of viewing the world through this map lens)?

Once students have viewed the three maps and placed sticky notes on the chart paper, they read their peers' responses then return to their groups to discuss how the maps may have influenced cultural beliefs and actions during this period. Students then write a paragraph providing opinions on what societal beliefs and actions may have been like during this time period. When defending answers, they should reference what they have discussed and seen in the maps. The teacher could hold onto these answers and pass the papers back to the students at the end of the Middle Ages unit for discussion on how accurate they were or to discuss what they would now change about their answers and why. We have provided an example from an eighth grade student's paragraph:

> Based on these three maps, I can tell that these people were very religious and that they believed in an afterlife. I know this because on each map there is a religious feature shown. On map one, there are four crosses surrounding the continents. On the second map, there is a box that reads "Paradise." Paradise is what people called the afterlife. I also

spotted multiple temples that they used as icons. I can also predict that these people are superstitious. The creature represents certain myths. Also, there are people that may serve a religious purpose. On the third map, no symbols nor icons were used. The icons that are on this map help me to know that these people believed highly in religion and worshipping certain religious figures.

This activity has several essential elements that fit into AMLE tenets in *This We Believe* (2010). It promotes active learning and provides a challenging curriculum. For example, throughout the activity, the multiple perspectives map example requires students to engage in hands-on, purposeful learning. This empowers them to explore and analyze the influence various experiences have on maps and the impact this has on perspectives.

 ## Diversity Activity in Civil Rights Class: Ruby Bridges

The activity begins by showing students the iconic Norman Rockwell painting of Ruby Bridges, *The Problem We All Live With* (the painting can be found at *http:// www.nrm.org/2012/08/new-perspectives-the-problem-we-all-live-with*). The teacher should not provide the students any background on the image. Students are given a few minutes to write down perceptions of the image. They are paired up to do a Venn Diagram comparing and contrasting their thoughts on the image. After five minutes, the teacher facilitates a classroom discussion about image perceptions. The teacher mentally takes note of the possible differences that diverse groups (e.g., based on race, gender, etc.) may have noted in their answers. These differences will be addressed later in the exercise.

After the discussion, the teacher reads *The Story of Ruby Bridges* (Coles & Ford, 1995) to the class. While reading, students should be thinking about the following focus questions:

- How did white people and African-Americans act differently?

- What are reasons different groups may have felt the way they did and acted the way they did in this story?

Students are then paired and briefly discuss and write answers to the aforementioned focus questions. Afterwards, there is a classroom discussion. The teacher should bring in the various perspectives that different students had about the painting shown earlier and have a discussion about individual experiences and how these influence our judgments and actions. Students then do an adaptation of the *Circles of My Multicultural Self activity* (Gorski, n.d.). On a piece of paper, they make a center circle with four satellite circles. Students write their names in the center circle and do the following:

1. Fill in each satellite circle with a dimension of their identity they consider to be among the most important in defining themselves. Some examples include female, athlete, their religion, and ethnicity.

2. Next, write a stereotype they have been treated as based on one dimension of their identity that fails to describe them accurately. Ask them to complete the following sentence by filling in the blanks: "I am (a/an) _____ but I am NOT (a/an) _____ ." Provide your own example, such as "I am a Muslim, but I am NOT a terrorist."

The teacher then asks for student volunteers to share the stereotypes and facilitates a class discussion about how it would feel to be treated like the stereotypes they have written and shared rather than be treated as an individual. Students finish by writing a paragraph about a time they have been treated as a stereotype and compare and contrast it with how Ruby Bridges may have felt. We have provided an example from the *Circles of My Multicultural Self* activity by a sixth grade student here:

> I have experienced stereotypical things about being tall, an athlete, and even funny similar to Ruby Bridge's treatment. For example, people have said that I should be embarrassed of being myself and being tall, which I'm not. I have also been told that I am dumb because I am an athlete, which is not true. I make all As and Bs in school. People should never judge others by a stereotype because it is not always true.

This activity fits into many of AMLE's characteristics through using varied learning approaches to explore multiple viewpoints. It provides different pedagogical approaches and a relevant curriculum that allows students to engage in meaningful self-reflection (AMLE, 2010). Through this activity, students are able to understand how their own experiences of being marginalized can be drawn upon to empathize and better understand what a person, such as Ruby Bridges may have been feeling during her experiences (Endacott & Brooks, 2013).

Teaching a Changing Historical Narrative

Perhaps the most important decision that we make as instructors is which themes and questions will frame our social studies courses. Readily accepted facts about U. S. history that are commonly believed among the American public and described in school texts may be disproven by research that uses primary sources (Zinn, 2003; Loewen, 2008). For this activity, we introduce a framework to teach about women's history that can be easily adapted to focus on a diverse array of groups. The framework has three activity sections. In the initial section, the dominant or traditional narrative of an event is shared. This is followed by the use of primary and secondary sources of the event, emphasizing the voice and eyes of a group not traditionally focused upon during the traditional narrative. The final section provides an in-depth analysis comparing the different narratives.

Using the framework, this example activity focuses on the American Civil War. The twist is the activity uses a female lens. To begin this activity, the instructor purposively teaches the traditional textbook narrative of the U.S. Civil War, which in most textbooks follows the single coherent story dominated by males (Loewen, 2008).

After students have received this traditional perspective, the teacher has the students write down their thoughts on women's roles during the U.S. Civil War and discuss these opinions. Next, give students the Women and the U.S. Civil War Data Chart (see Figure 4.4). Students will work in pairs to investigate primary and secondary sources of female life before and during the civil war and fill in the chart. They may be surprised to discover that there were women who played critical roles as soldiers, nurses, doctors, and spies. With so many men away, women also took on critical roles during this period in professions previously dominated by men, such as taking over family businesses and plantations.

Figure 4.4 *Women and the U.S. Civil War Data Chart*

Pre-U.S. Civil War/ During U.S. Civil War	Female Role	Summary of Role Described	Benefits/ Opportunities for Women Role Provides

Figure 4.5 provides links and summaries of possible websites for students to use. It is recommended that the sources be divided up after students have been provided time to analyze the documents and fill in their charts. The teacher facilitates a class discussion and puts student answers in a larger version of the data chart on butcher paper.

Figure 4.5 *Women Roles Sites*

Women's Lives Before U.S. Civil War *(http://edsitement.neh.gov/lesson-plan/womens-lives-civil-war#sect-activities)*: Provides information on how women's lives had been changing in the U.S. in the 1850s. Examples include the abolitionist movement, authors, and speaking out for women's rights.
Women Soldiers of the U.S. Civil War *(http://www.archives.gov/publications/prologue/1993/spring/women-in-the-civil-war-1.html)*: Provides individual and group stories of women as soldiers fighting in the Civil War.
Women in the U.S. Civil War: Ladies, Contraband, Spies *(http://www.loc.gov/teachers/classroommaterials/lessons/women-cw/gallery.html)*: A collection of primary source documents of women's lives and roles during the U.S. Civil War era.

At the conclusion of this class discussion, students write an alternative U.S. Civil War textbook entry (100-150 words) with females as the dominant protagonists. They edit their entries and then share them in small groups and discuss the following questions.

- How would a textbook with this different perspective impact your reading of the U.S. Civil War?

- How did your new textbook entries change your perspective on female roles during U.S. Civil War time period?

This activity framework fits into an array of AMLE's essential attributes. For example, the framework provides equity by giving a curriculum that looks at multiple sides of a story. It is empowering for students, enabling them to explore history through the eyes of her own gender and ethnicity. Students are challenged through engaging and purposeful active learning activities that require them to hypothesize and advocate for perspectives not traditionally taught (NMSA, 2010).

Conclusion

Our middle schools continue to become increasingly diverse, and it is critical that we broaden our pedagogical repertoire to meet the needs of all students. The best practices outlined in this chapter fit squarely in the AMLE essential attributes of being developmentally responsive, challenging, and equitable (NMSA, 2010). Social studies is a discipline rich in perspectives. By focusing on the diverse learners that make up each middle school classroom, teachers increase learning for every student while establishing a classroom environment of rigor and depth that can lead to an increased respect for others.

Additional Resources

National Association for Multicultural Education *(http://www.nameorg.org)*: This non-profit organization advocates for equity and social justice through multicultural education. The website provides information on the organization, its state affiliates, multicultural education conferences, publications, and classroom resources.

Zinn Education Project *(http://zinnedproject.org)*: The Zinn Education Project promotes and supports the use of Howard Zinn's best-selling book, *A People's History of the United States*, provides insights on misinformation in social studies textbooks, and gives other materials for teaching social studies in middle and high school classrooms. The website offers free resources for classroom teachers.

Teaching Tolerance (*http://www.tolerance.org*): Teaching Tolerance attempts to combat prejudice and promotes equality, inclusiveness, and equitable learning environments in the classroom. The website has award winning classroom documentaries, lesson plans, and other classroom resources, including publications promoting diversity in the classroom.

Teaching Channel: Teacher's Toolkit for ELL (*https://www.teachingchannel. org/blog/2014/11/04/english-language-learners-resources*): This blog on The Teaching Channel is a space for educators to provide resources and tips for working with ELL students. Resources include best practices, lesson ideas and strategies, and tips for planning to teach ELL students. Additionally, a space is provided for questions that teachers may have working with this population.

National Women's History Project (*http://www.nwhp.org*): This program focuses on revising the standard curriculum to give women fair recognition of their role in history. The website provides resources and educational materials on the historic accomplishments of an array of women.

National Women's History Museum (*https://www.nwhm.org/online-exhibits*): Students explore women's history with these hands-on digital exhibits and accompanying lesson plans. Additionally, there are a number of other valuable resources, including biographies, videos, and interactive activities.

Museum of Disability History (*http://museumofdisability.org*): This museum is dedicated to educating the public about people with disabilities. Lesson plans and a virtual museum are among the resources available.

National Association for Gifted Children (*http://www.nagc.org*): This website provides resources, publications, and a community for educators and parents on teaching and raising gifted and talented students. Information on professional development opportunities in this area is also available on the website.

References

Bailey, S. (2004) Types of acceleration and their effectiveness. In core module 6: Developing programs and provisions for gifted students. In Stan Bailey, Miraca Gross, Bronwyn MacLeod, Graham Chaffey, Ruth Targett and Caroline Merrick. *Professional development package for teachers in gifted education.* Canberra, Australia: Department of Education, Science and Training.

Banks, J. A. (2004). Multicultural education: Characteristics and goals. In J. A. Banks & C. A. McGee Banks (Eds.), *Multicultural education: Issues and perspectives* (3-30). Hoboken, NJ: Wiley.

Barton, K., & Levstik, L. (2004). *Teaching history for the common good.* Mahwah, NJ: Lawrence Erlbaum Associates, Inc.

Belknap, N. J., & Hess, E. K. (2000). The conversation begins with us: Exploring the prejudice in our thinking. *Reclaiming Children and Youth, 9*(1), 25-28; 40.

Bos, C. S. & Vaughn, S. (2006). *Strategies for teaching students with learning and behavior problems.* Boston, MA: Allyn and Bacon.

Chick, K., & Heilman-Houser, R. (2000). Children's literature choices: Gender stereotypes prevail. *Pennsylvania Reads: Journal of the Keystone State Reading Association, 1*(2), 3-13.

Coles, R., & Ford, G. C. (1995). *The story of Ruby Bridges.* New York, NY: Scholastic.

Cruz, B. C. & Thornton, S. J. (2008). Social studies for all: ESOL strategies for the elementary classroom. *Social Studies and the Young Learner, 21*(2), 11-16.

Davis, G. A., & Rimm, S. B. (1998). *Education of the gifted and talented* (4th ed.). Needham Heights, MA: Allyn & Bacon.

Diaz, E. I. (1998). Perceived factors influencing the academic underachievement of talented students of Puerto Rican descent. *Gifted Child Quarterly, 42*, 105–122.

Endacott, J. & Brooks, S. (2013). An updated theoretical and practical model for promoting historical empathy. *Social Studies Research and Practice 8*(1), 41-57.

Etlin, M. (1988). To teach them all is to know them all. *NEA Today*, 10-11.

Fitchett, P. G. & Heafner, T. L. (2012). Culturally responsive social studies teaching: Models of theory into practice. In W. B. Russell III (Ed.), *Contemporary social studies: An essential reader* (195-214). Charlotte, NC: Information Age Publishing Inc.

Gay, G. (2002). Preparing for culturally responsive teaching. *Journal of Teacher Education, 53*(2), 106-116.

Gorski, P. C. (n.d.). *Circles of my multicultural self.* Retrieved from http://www.edchange. org/multicultural/activities/circlesofself_handout.htm.

Jaffee, A. T. (2016). Community, voice and inquiry: Teaching global history for English language learners. *The Social Studies, 107*(3), 89-101.

Kaplan, L. S. (1990). *Helping gifted students with stress management.* Reston, VA: The International Council for Exceptional Children.

Kena, G., Aud, S., Johnson, F., Wang, X., Zhang, J., Rathbun, A., Wilkinson-Flicker, S., & Kristapovich, P. (2014). *The condition of education 2014* (NCES 2014-083). U.S. Department of Education, National Center for Education Statistics. Washington, DC. Retrieved from http://nces.ed.gov/pubsearch.

Krashen S. D., & Terrell, T. D. (1983). *The natural approach: Language acquisition in the classroom.* Hayward, CA: The Alemany Press.

Libresco, A. S. & Balantic, J. (2013). Nurturing students' analytical skills with primary sources: A women's history case study. *The Oregon Journal of the Social Studies, 1*(1), 58-68.

Loewen, J. W. (2008). *Lies my teacher told me: Everything your American history textbook got wrong.* New York, NY: New Press.

Maker, C. J. (1987). Gifted and talented. In V. Richardson-Koehler (Ed.), *Educators' handbook: A research perspective* (420-456). White Plains, NY: Longman.

McCabe, J., Fairchild, E. Grauerholz, L. Pescosolido, B. A., & Tope, D. (2011). Gender in twentieth-century children's books patters of disparity in titles and central characters. *Gender & Society, 25*(2), 197-226.

Mercer, C. D., & Mercer, A. R. (2005). *Teaching students with learning problems.* Upper Saddle River, NJ: Prentice Hall.

Minarik, D. & Lintner, T. (2016). *Social studies and exceptional learners.* NCSS Bulletin 115. Silver Spring, MD: NCSS.

National Assessment of Educational Progress [NAEP]. (2015). *The Nation's Report Card.* Retrieved from https://nces.ed.gov/pubsearch/pubsinfo.asp?pubid=2015112.

NMSA. (2010). *This we believe: Keys to educating young adolescents*. Westerville, OH: Author.

Peck, C. (2010). "It's not like [I'm] Chinese and Canadian. I Am in between": Ethnicity and students' conceptions of historical significance. *Theory and Research in Social Education, 38*(4), 575-617.

Rayneri, L. J., Gerber, B. L., & Wiley, L. P. (2006). The relationship between classroom environment and the learning style preferences of gifted middle school student and the impact on levels of performance. *Gifted Child Quarterly, 50*(2), 104-118.

Seeley, K. (2004). Gifted and talented students at risk. *Focus on Exceptional Children, 37*(4), 1-8.

Scheiner-Fisher, C. & Russell, W. B. (2012). Using historical films to promote gender equity in the history curriculum. *The Social Studies, 103*(6), 221-225.

Steele, M. M. (2007). Teaching social studies to high school students with learning problems. *The Social Studies, 98*(2), 59-63.

Todd, S. (2011). Educating beyond cultural diversity: Redrawing the boundaries of a democratic plurality. *Studies in Philosophy and Education, 30*(2), 101-111.

Ukpokodu, O. N. (2003). Meeting the needs of diverse learners. *Social Studies and the Young Learner, 16*(1), 31-32.

U.S. Department of Education. (2015). *English language learners*. Retrieved from http://nces.ed.gov/programs/coe/indi cator_cgf.asp.

Woyshner, C. (2012). Gender and social studies: Are we there yet? In W. B. Russell III Ed.), *Contemporary social studies: An essential reader* (261-276). Charlotte, NC: Information Age Publishing Inc.

Yoder, P. J., Kibler, A., & van Hover, S. (2016). Instruction for English language learners in the social studies classroom: A meta-synthesis. *Social Studies Research and Practice, 11*(1), 20-39.

Zine, J. (2002). Inclusive schooling in a plural society: Removing the margins. *Education Canada, 42*(3), 1-4.

Zinn, H. (2003). *A people's history of the United States*. 1492-Present (Perennial ed.). New York, NY: Harper.

05

Social Studies as a Learning Quest: Adventures in Research

The National Council for the Social Studies (NCSS) and the Association for Middle Level Education (AMLE) stress that the transition for students from elementary to middle school is fraught with physical, social, and emotional changes (NCSS, 1991; NMSA, 2010). One of these changes is the complexity of reading materials. Many students are overwhelmed by these more rigorous literacy expectations. Social studies teachers must be mindful of this reality and design instruction to enable students to successfully work with different types of reading materials.

There are many different types of literature that can be used in the middle school social studies classroom. This chapter does not attempt to catalogue and describe all types of texts that could be used. Instead, we focus on three kinds of reading materials: primary sources, content-area picture books, and graphic novels. Examples are provided for texts along with a classroom activity for each. Two appendices are provided that contain additional classroom activities and example texts.

The Function of Texts in the Social Studies

What is a carpenter without a hammer and saw? These are the tools of this trade. For a social scientist, the necessary working tools are inked on paper, etched on stone, and electronically transmitted. Social scientists must examine these for arguments, biases, and perspectives of people from different times and cultures. All of these processes allow them to construct historical arguments (Carr, 1961). Along the way to constructing a historical argument, consideration should be given to texts about a topic with competing arguments and perspectives. It is important to remember that people's views are directly influenced by their cultural, regional, and political values. This means many will perceive the same event, issue, or person very differently (Clabough, Turner, Russell, & Waters, 2016).

An understanding of a social scientist's job is germane given the current educational reform movements such as the C3 Framework by NCSS (NCSS, 2013). This reform document places an emphasis on building students' content-area literacy skills by having them critically scrutinize texts. It argues that students should be able to analyze the author's point of views and biases. These skills are vital in the 21st century given the bombardment of social, cultural, and political messages that students are exposed to on a daily basis.

Benefits of a Text-Driven Middle School Social Studies Classroom

There are several benefits to having a text-driven middle school social studies classroom. First, high-quality reading materials make for more compelling reads. The historical figures in our curriculums become more three dimensional in the minds of our students because we see them from their account books and ledgers to their love letters to the documents that made them great (Endacott & Brooks, 2013). These texts are like the tabloids in the checkout lane at the grocery store: they make students want to know the whole story.

Second, the types of readings we are referencing set up the potential for more meaningful classroom discussions. The readings provoke students to want to share their thoughts on a topic. This lets the teacher use open-ended questions to delve deeper into a topic. For example, an exploration of *Common Sense* by Thomas Paine permits students to analyze the conflict among colonials about the growing tension with Great Britain. It also shows the masterful ways that Paine constructs an argument. Paine clearly, eloquently, and succinctly contends that the colonies should sever their ties with Great Britain. The teacher can set up a research activity for students to pursue Paine's logic. For example, students may investigate his argument for the ease in which the colonies could build a navy. Such an activity can only build students' own ability to construct an argument and position (Giles, Wang, Smith, & Johnson, 2013).

Third, high-quality reading materials allow teachers to meet the different learning styles of our students. A wide range of reading materials presents the opportunity for students to work with texts of different difficulty and style. For example, a graphic novel appeals to visual learners, struggling readers, and ESL students. The pages of a graphic novel contain less text and more images, which makes it easier for these groups of students to construct meaning (Sheffield, Chisholm, & Howell, 2015). However, oral materials such as FDR's Fireside Chats appeal to students who learn better through listening. Our pedagogy must be adaptable to meet the diverse learning needs of our students.

Our Recommended Types of Texts

At this point, it is fair to ask, "What types of texts are being recommended?" Our focus in the remaining sections of this chapter is on primary sources, content-area picture books, and graphic novels. We provide best practice examples from each. It is important for teachers to remember that students may not enter middle school classrooms with the pre-requisite skills to analyze the three selected text categories. Therefore, our example activities also contain recommendations for helping students grasp the elements within each text category.

Primary Sources

The definition of primary sources is not something that fits neatly in a box. Primary sources include everything from newspapers to scrapbooks to garbage piles. They are the remnants from previous time periods that were preserved by design or chance and allow us to contextualize issues, values, and beliefs by reading the words of people during a historical era (Vest, 2005). The best way to approach how we look at primary sources with students begins with some sort of categorization. For our purposes, we will focus on the two most commonly used categories: text-based and visual primary sources.

Text-based Primary Sources

The category with the most prolific number of primary sources is text based. Text-based primary sources include all forms of the written word directly from an era. These include diaries, government records, personal correspondences, and speeches. The biases, values, and beliefs of individuals are often expressed in text-based primary sources. Biases take many forms ranging from loaded language to fact stacking (Austin & Thompson, 2015). Students need to be able to critically explore the perspectives within a source. Since students often come to our classes lacking these skills, the teacher needs to model and discuss how they can analyze the components within a text-based primary source.

Deconstructing a Primary Source with a Word Web

The example graphic organizer in Figure 5.1 was completed by an eighth grade student. The completion of this graphic organizer is one way teachers can help students analyze perspectives in text-based primary sources. This type of graphic organizer allows students to explore all of the factors connected to a term, phrase, individual, or event. The class activity involves groups of three. The example shows three levels. The first level has students define and describe the title of the source, in this case Pope Urban II's speech that initiated the Crusades. The speech can be found at *http://legacy.fordham.edu/Halsall/source/urban2-5vers.asp#Fulcher.* The second level enables students to focus on the language of that speech, especially the phrases and sentences that Pope Urban II used to make his argument. The third level permits students to articulate the meaning of his words used in level two.

Figure 5.1 *Student Word Web for One Version of Pope Urban II's Speech*

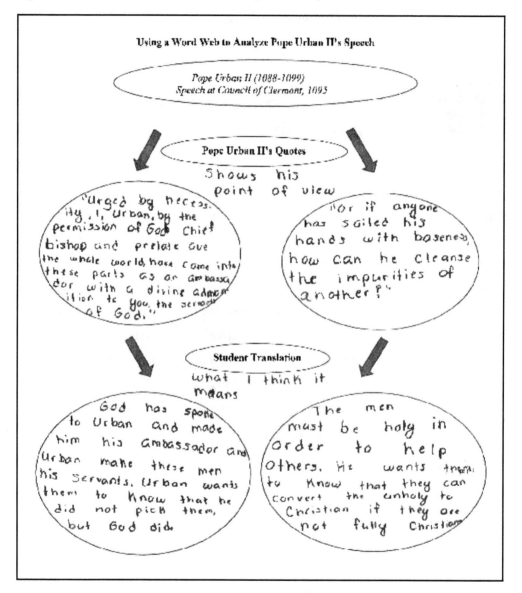

Using a Word Web to Analyze Pope Urban II's Speech

Pope Urban II (1088-1099)
Speech at Council of Clermont, 1095

Pope Urban II's Quotes

Shows his point of view

"Urged by necessity, I, Urban, by the permission of God, Chief bishop and prelate over the whole world, have come into these parts as an ambassador with a divine admonition to you, the servant of God."

"For if anyone has soiled his hands with baseness, how can he cleanse the impurities of another?"

Student Translation

what I think it means

God has spoke to Urban and made him his Ambassador and Urban make these men his servants. Urban wants them to know that he did not pick them, but God did.

The men must be holy in order to help others. He wants them to know that they can convert the unholy to Christian if they are not fully Christian.

Obviously, more boxes should be added to the second and third level to fully explore the speech. The teacher should float around the room to help students with this activity. This particular speech was selected because of its extensive use of persuasive language that contributed to people joining an actual Crusade. Factors include the status of the Pope's power during this period to the prevalence of pilgrimages to holy lands for atonement to the number of second sons that saw they could fiscally benefit by carving out a new fiefdom for themselves.

After the groups complete this graphic organizer, there should be a debriefing. Groups need to share their findings while the teacher guides this discussion. Follow-up questions can be asked to get students to elaborate on their selected terms or phrases in the second level of this graphic organizer. Some questions may include why do you think the author of a primary source uses a certain phrase, or how might that phrase influence a person's actions? Students need to add to their word web while listening to their peers' comments.

This process can lead to writing activities where students answer open-ended questions about the effectiveness of the persuasive language in this speech. One open-ended question that a teacher might use is, "Do you think that this speech persuaded people to take part in the Crusades and if so for what reasons?" By answering this question, students can explore how Pope Urban II appealed to people throughout Europe during the 11th century to take part in the Crusades. The examination of the reasons that people took part in the Crusades ultimately enables students to better contextualize the beliefs and biases of individuals during this time period.

The completion of this activity gives students experience analyzing the components of text-based primary sources. These processes need to be completed multiple times to give students practice and experience with these kinds of analysis skills. To critically engage in a dialogue with the author of a primary source, students must be able to examine the words in a document. These words and phrases are clues to help students better understand the purposes for creating a primary source (Wineburg, Martin, & Monte-Sano, 2012). It is the critical examination of social studies topics in this manner that enables students to dig deeper into the material (NMSA, 2010).

 ## Visual Primary Sources

Visual primary sources are images preserved from history in the forms of photographs, lithographs, paintings, and political cartoons. With these kinds of sources, students must grasp how the artist or photographer uses imagery to convey ideas and how symbolism is used within these sources. It is also important that students understand the purposes for creating such primary sources (Waters & Russell, 2013). Most of the time a visual primary source has been preserved for particular purposes. We must help students uncover the messages within these sources. This is particularly true of political cartoons.

Political cartoons have long been a staple in American society. They are used to convey ideas and influence people's opinions about a topic. One of the most famous political cartoons is Ben Franklin's "Join or Die." Created in the French and Indian War, this drawing was later used to convey the need for unity among the colonies in the face of conflict against Great Britain.

The teacher can have students explore the elements of Franklin's political cartoon in pairs by providing students with background knowledge about the relationships among the British colonies and then ask students to consider why this political cartoon became connected so closely to the cause of American independence. After analyzing and discussing this primary source, the students could then assume the roles of colonists that support unity against Great Britain and write an op-ed piece.

By an op-ed piece, we are referring to short essays that people write to share their opinions about a topic. Op-ed pieces combine elements of perspective and persuasive writing to convince people about a point of view related to specific issues and events. The length of this writing piece needs to be a paragraph and should contain evidence from class discussion along with the ideas represented in Franklin's political cartoon. We have provided an example op-ed piece below.

Example Op-Ed Piece for Colonial Unity

Brothers, Mr. Franklin's cartoon contains a message of unity that we must follow. While we may have our differences, it is important that we unite against a common enemy that threatens the rights and liberties that we hold dear: Great Britain. I know many of those among us still perceive Great Britain as a loving parent. However, would a caring parent engage in repeated injuries that sap the vitality from our political process or trample on the political privileges that we enjoy as free men? It is time that we put aside our differences and repel our common foe that strikes at the very fabric of the values that we hold dear.

The students should then share their op-ed pieces. The teacher needs to ask questions to encourage students to articulate the reasons for phrasing their ideas in a specific manner. Some of these questions might include:

- Why do you think that the ideas in your op-ed piece will contribute to colonial unity?

- How did you frame your argument against Great Britain?

These questions not only help students unpack their thinking but enable them to see how people formulate arguments.

This activity enables students to explore the concept of messaging in a political cartoon. Students are analyzing and discussing the message of "Join or Die" and then applying that content knowledge to create an op-ed piece (Bickford, 2012). This activity permits students to explore how individuals and groups use imagery to persuade others. In the 21st century, people are bombarded by visuals that attempt to influence their every decision. These influences range from apparel to purchase to food to eat to television shows to watch. It is important that students are able to decode the messages within visual primary sources to make responsible decisions (Engle & Ochoa, 1988).

Content-Area Picture Books

Content-area picture books are a great source to explore historical figures and events in more depth. Many books in this genre give a great sense of the personality of historical figures and capture the feel of an event. The two most prominent types are biographical and event-based content-area picture books.

Biographical Content-area Picture Books

Biographical content-area picture books allow students to explore the personality, actions, and perspectives with both well-known and obscure historical figures (Wooten, 2000). Through reading these books, students can gain more insight into historical figures and empathize with a person's struggles, choices, and decisions.

Biographical content-area picture books tend to be short in length. The teacher can usually read one in a lesson plan transition. We model a possible activity with a biographical content-area picture book using *A Splash of Red: The Life and Art of Horace Pippin* (Bryant, 2013). *A Splash of Red* provides a biography of Horace Pippins life. The author also subtly discusses more abstract concepts such as overcoming adversity to accomplish one's dreams. It took Pippin two years to paint his first piece after losing the use of his right hand in World War I. This fact can lead to some powerful class discussions.

Using Biographic Content-Area Picture Books to Set up Student Research

The teacher should start off by reading *A Splash of Red*. Class read alouds have the potential to improve our students' vocabulary and writing skills (Layne, 2015). As the teacher reads *A Splash of Red*, students should be thinking about the style of Horace Pippin's paintings. They need to then discuss his paintings shown in this book. The teacher should ask questions that focus students' attention on the features of pop art. Some of these questions may include what message is the artist trying to convey, and what does the painting capture about an event?

The teacher will then set up research activities about Pippin's paintings for students to complete in pairs. The back of this book contains a map showing where Pippin's paintings are on display. When designing activities with biographical content-area picture books, it is important to let the contents of the book guide the direction of your classroom activities. The pairs can research one of these paintings and complete the painting analysis questions below.

Painting Analysis Sheet for Horace Pippin's Painting

- What is the subject of your selected painting, and where is it located?

- How does the color used in the painting add to its meaning?

- What aspects of life is the painting trying to capture?

- Why do you think that Pippin created your chosen painting?

After the pairs answer these questions, they share their findings. This gives students the opportunity to learn from their peers while taking ownership of their learning as they research and explore Pippin's pop art. It also reflects the emphasis in AMLE's *This We Believe* on student-centered learning (NMSA, 2010). Our students cannot be passive observers in our classroom. Instead, they must be actively involved in every step of the learning process.

It must also be emphasized that this activity strengthens the classroom learning environment. Our students, whether they admit it or not, enjoy being read to in class. Read alouds can help contribute to a stronger learning community (Trelease, 2013). Teachers must work to build this type of environment to create meaningful learning opportunities.

Event-based Content-Area Picture Books

Some content-area picture books attempt to explore historical events in more depth. These books examine the perspective of an individual or group about an event. This level of scrutiny permits students to see different perspectives about an event.

The teacher can do a read aloud for *Brave Girl: Clara and the Shirtwaist Makers' Strike of 1909* (Markel, 2013) as a starting point for students to explore labor disputes at the beginning of the 20th century. *Brave Girl* chronicles the conditions that led to the Shirtwaist Makers' Strike of 1909 and Clara Lemlich's role in this event. While the teacher is reading this book aloud, students should jot down examples of reasons why people may have felt compelled to go on strike and then share their thoughts.

The students then explore the conditions that led to other strikes during this time period. The teacher should split the students into groups of three and have each group research the working conditions that led to labor disputes. Some topics may include the Haymarket Affair, Homestead Strike, and Pullman Strike. The teacher needs to provide websites about these topics.

After students have completed their research, the groups create their own content-area picture book. It should focus on the group's researched labor dispute. Each group's book needs to convey the main ideas and details that led to a labor dispute from the perspective of the labor union.

This activity builds students' research skills as they explore the working conditions that lead to labor disputes. The compelling question of examining working conditions in the Gilded Age and Progressive Era enables students to see this issue from labor unions' perspectives. The ability to empathize with the values and beliefs of people from the past allows students to contextualize issues during a time period (Levstik & Barton, 2015). All of these processes reflect the type of meaningful interactions with our content material that AMLE's *This We Believe* stresses should happen in our classrooms (NMSA, 2010).

Graphic Novels

A graphic novel can be thought of as a cousin to the comic book. It uses both images and words to convey information. However, the events and issues explored in this form of literature tend to be more mature in nature (Carano & Clabough, 2016). Graphic novels use a combination of words, images, thought/speech balloons, and facial expressions to convey thoughts and ideas about a topic (Botzakis, 2015). Most tend to take one of two forms: event-based graphic novels or bio-graphic novels.

Event-based Graphic Novels

Event-based graphic novels try to capture in chronological order the sequence of historic events around a central topic. Some examples of event-based graphic novels include *The 9/11 Report: A Graphic Adaptation* (Jacobson, 2006) and *The United States Constitution: A Graphic Adaptation* (Hennessey, 2008).

 ## Page Analysis Activity for Graphic Novels

One activity that the teacher can use to help students become familiar with *March Book Two* or any other graphic novel of this type is an individual page analysis. *March Book Two* focuses on John Lewis' experiences during the Civil Rights Movement. John Lewis was an active participant in many pivotal events of the Civil Rights Movement. He took part in the Freedom Rides, assumed a leadership role in the Selma March, and spoke at the March on Washington. This graphic novel also does an excellent job of chronicling major events of the movement including the Freedom Rides and the Children's March (Lewis & Aydin, 2015).

One activity that the teacher can use to help students become familiar with the components of this and any other graphic novel is to do an individual page analysis. The teacher selects a page from *March Book Two*. She then creates a visual aide containing the same panel layout of the graphic novel page. Page 132 from *March Book Two* focuses on the Children's March in Birmingham. The teacher needs to introduce the visual aide by analyzing the first panel on this page. She may provide some questions to spark discussion and to highlight that this first panel provides information about the coordination within the African American community for protests. Some sample questions may include the following: What role did the 16th Street Baptist Church play in organizing events? What role did radio stations play in the Civil Rights Movement? Why would civil rights activists use coded language in announcements? The students should take notes with everything happening in this panel. This process should be duplicated with the other panels on the page. We have provided some possible questions for the remaining panels below.

Questions for *March Book Two*

Panels Two, Three, and Four on Page 132

- How are civil rights activists portrayed in these panels?

- What characteristics would you use to describe the civil rights activists in these panels?

- Why did the artist include panel three with the car tire?

Panels Five through Eight on Page 132

- Why does the artist depict the cop in the manner demonstrated in panels five and seven?

- How does the presence of the police change the mood of the protest movement in Birmingham?

- Why does the artist focus on the young civil rights activists' face in panels six and eight?

Student pairs then complete the rest of the page layout worksheet about this page in *March Book Two* by focusing on the reasons the comic book artist depicts certain images in each panel. Many times artists use symbolism within their images (Boerman-Cornell 2015).

After completing the assignment, students share their findings. The teacher should guide this discussion by getting students to articulate key concepts within these panels. For example, she may ask students, "Why does the young African American male appear to be sweating on panels six and eight?" The class should discuss each panel, and then, students would take some time to answer the following open-ended question in a paragraph. What is the author trying to convey on this page about the Children's March? The students will want to discuss key content material covered along with the symbolism of imagery in this page. They need to use evidence from this graphic novel page in their paragraphs. Below is an example paragraph.

Example Summary of page 132
from *March Book Two*

> This page of the graphic novel discusses how people in the African American community in Birmingham got organized to protest. These people used the radio along with central meeting places in their communities. They are shown peacefully protesting. The cops depicted on this page do not seem friendly. The artist takes three panels to show the young African American male's fear of the cop while taking part in the Children's March. He does this by showing the sweat on the young boy's brow with panels six and eight.

The students should then share their paragraphs. The teacher needs to get students to unpack their thinking. This class discussion and activity allow students to gain experience working with graphic novels. The teacher will want to repeat this process multiple times to enable students to feel comfortable working with graphic novels.

This activity lets students get in the mind of the graphic novel artist to see how he or she constructs meaning. Through this activity, students gain the knowledge to work with the literacy devices contained within a graphic novel. These literacy devices are especially useful given that some of our students are not reading on grade level, and English is not the first language for some (Brozo, Moorman, & Meyer, 2014).

Bio-graphic Novels

The second type of graphic novel focuses on the personalities, accomplishments, and shortcomings of historical figures. Bio-graphic novels tend to provide a chronological narrative about a specific individual. The company, Hill and Wang, has produced several of these graphic novels including *Ronald Reagan: A Graphic Biography* (Helfer, 2007) and *Malcolm X: A Graphic Biography* (Helfer, 2006).

The teacher can use any graphic novel of this type to do an in-depth character analysis of a historical figure. We will use *Ronald Reagan: A Graphic Biography* (Helfer, 2007) as a model. The teacher should have students in small groups read this graphic novel in segments. With each reading segment, the students should keep a journal. The layout of these journal notes can be determined by the student based on his or her learning preferences. Below is an example of what students' notes might look like for pages 59-65.

Example of Journal from pages 59-65 of Ronald Reagan

- Reagan has a tendency to make some silly mistakes in public like getting the age wrong for President Giscard D'Estaing.

- His homespun nature played well with a portion of the American public. This can be seen in his interactions with John Breen during a Republican primary debate.

- He did not always have substantial knowledge about events. This can be seen by Reagan asking President Carter for note cards during their meetings.

- Reagan's inaugural address contained issues that mattered to him. These issues included lowering taxes, expanding the military, and defeating Communism.

After the students complete a reading segment in this graphic novel, they should share their journal entries. This enables students to articulate their understanding of this content material. The teacher can clarify any student misunderstandings.

After students finish reading this graphic novel, they should complete a character profile for Ronald Reagan. The character profile technique is often used in comic books and graphic novels to convey the essence of a character by describing his or her attributes, personality, and beliefs. With this activity, students create a comic page capturing essential ideas and values for Reagan from their journal entries and class discussion. They should use different literacy skills contained within graphic novels. These include text boxes, thought bubbles, and symbolic imagery. Their character profile page should capture Reagan's personality.

Students should then share their character profile page. They need to highlight the reasons for including certain items as well as how those reflect certain aspects of Reagan's character as well as how certain segments of the population viewed him. The teacher facilitates this sharing by asking students to explain different elements within their character profile page.

This activity allows students to examine a historical figure in depth. Students are able to see Reagan in three dimensional terms by exploring all aspects of his life (Clark, 2014). With the character profile page, they have to capture Reagan's personality and values. This enables students to demonstrate their understanding of content material from this graphic novel. Through graphic novels, the beliefs espoused by historical figures become meaningful and relevant in the minds of our students. *This We Believe* stresses this is the type of active engagement with our content material that students need (NMSA, 2010). This type of analysis of the past is necessary if the people from the pages of history are to resonate with our students. Figure 5.2 is an example of a possible character profile page for Reagan.

Figure 5.2 *Example Character Profile Page for Ronald Reagan*

Conclusion

This chapter focused on three types of high quality texts that have the potential to engage and deepen our students' thinking with social studies topics: primary sources, content-area picture books, and graphic novels. All three types of texts contain the content material in our state standards. The teacher needs to model and design activities with the literacy devices used in these three types of texts. The activities in the chapter are designed to provide examples for how this may be done. By using these types of texts, the teacher is preparing students for the more rigorous literacy expectations in middle school social studies classrooms. More importantly, students gain literacy skills to decode messaging through the written word, images, and media advertising. These literacy skills help students function and make informed decisions in the 21st century.

Additional Resources

Farrell, M. (2014). *Pure grit: How American World War II nurses survived battle and prison camp in the Pacific*. New York, NY: Abrams

A great trade book for exploring POW nurses' experiences during World War II is *Pure Grit: How American World War II Nurses Survived Battle and Prison Camp in the Pacific* (Farrell, 2014). Teachers can have students explore abstract concepts with this trade book such as courage, honor, and duty to one's country. After reading selected chapters, students can assume the role of one of the POW nurses and write a journal entry about her daily life. By completing this activity, they can empathize with the emotional and physical toll of the POW nurses' service.

Demi. (2012). *Columbus*. Las Vegas, NV: Amazon Publishing

Demi's books are great content-area picture books to use in the world history classroom. Most provide biographies for famous people in world history. An ideal example is *Columbus* (Demi, 2012). It gives a balanced overview of Columbus' accomplishments and shortcomings. The teacher may utilize *Columbus* for students to gain a better understanding of the various dimensions of this historical figure's actions and his impact on the world. He can have students complete a graphic organizer about certain items discussed in Demi's *Columbus*. These topics may include Columbus' treatment of native tribes in the "New World" and his joy of exploration. Students then share their findings. This activity allows students to gain a better understanding about the complexity of Columbus.

Sheinkin, S. (2014). *The Port Chicago 50: Disaster, mutiny, and the fight for civil rights*. New York, NY: Roaring Brook Press.

Another author with high-quality books for exploring social studies topics is Steve Sheinkin. All of Sheinkin's books are well researched and contain numerous primary sources about a topic. For example, *The Port Chicago 50: Disaster, Mutiny, and the Fight for Civil Rights* (Sheinkin, 2014) focuses on the mutiny trial of 50 African American sailors that refused to go back to an unsafe work environment after an accident at a shipyard cost the lives of over 300 Americans. Students may read the chapters in this book that explore the trial evidence. They could then assume the role of Thurgood Marshall and write a statement to release to the press about the injustices of this trial related to civil rights issues. The length of the students' press release needs to be a paragraph. This perspective-writing activity enables students to capture Marshall's feelings about this particular trial.

Rappaport, D. (2015). *Frederick's journey: The life of Frederick Douglass*. New York, NY: Jump at the Sun.

Doreen Rappaport has amazing content-area picture books that can be used in U.S. history. Rappaport's books use the book narrative, quotes from the subject of her book, and images to capture the essence of famous U.S. historical figures. Her most recent book, *Frederick's Journey: The Life of Frederick Douglass* (Rappaport,

2015), focuses on the abolitionist's thoughts, hopes, and dreams. Students can read this book and analyze the quotes from Douglass included throughout the book. They should complete a graphic organizer in pairs discussing the central ideas in Douglass' quotes. The next step in this activity is to create fake quotes that Frederick Douglass would say about issues in his time period. With this activity, students are applying content knowledge learned about Douglass and attempting to capture his quintessential beliefs. They should write a paragraph explaining how their quote captures the values of Frederick Douglass.

Bausum, A. (2012). *Marching to the mountaintop: How poverty, labor fights and civil rights set the stage for Martin Luther King Jr.'s final hours.* Washington D.C.: National Geographic.

National Geographic has a lot of high-quality books that contain emotionally-charged black and white photographs and powerful narratives about topics in U.S. history. Anne Bausum has several powerful trade books by National Geographic. One book that may be utilized from this author is *Marching to the Mountaintop: How Poverty, Labor Fights, and Civil Rights Set the Stage for Martin Luther King Jr.'s Final Hours* (Bausum, 2012). Students can read and discuss the contents of this book to see why Dr. King took up the cause of sanitation workers in Memphis. They can then create a plan for protesting the treatment of these workers. Their plans should include steps for their actions along with realistic goals to accomplish. This activity builds students' problem solving skills.

Content-Area Picture Books

Brown, D. (2013). *Henry and the cannons: An extraordinary true story of the American Revolution.* New York, NY: Roaring Brook Press.

Fritz, J. (2013). *Alexander Hamilton: The outsider.* New York, NY: G.P. Putnam's Sons.

Nelson, V. (2009). *Bad news for outlaws: The remarkable life of Bass Reeves, deputy U.S. marshal.* Minneapolis, MN: Carolrhoda Books.

Graphic Novels

Lewis, J. & Aydin, A. (2013). *March book one*. Marietta, GA: Top Shelf Productions.

Hale, N. (2012). *Nathan Hale's hazardous tales: One dead spy*. New York, NY: Abrams.

Spiegelman, A. (1986). *Maus I: A survivor's tale: My father bleeds*. New York, NY: Pantheon.

Hennessey, J. (2008). *The United States Constitution: A graphic adaptation*. New York, NY: Hill and Wang.

Primary Source Websites

Social Studies Central:
http://www.socialstudiescentral.com/instructional-resources/primary-sources

American Rhetoric: *http://www.americanrhetoric.com*

Famous Trials: *http://law2.umkc.edu/faculty/projects/ftrials/ftrials.htm*

Eyewitness to History: *http://www.eyewitnesstohistory.com*

Historical Scene Investigation: *http://www.hsionline.org*

References

Austin, H. & Thompson, K. (2015). *Examining the evidence: Seven strategies for teaching with primary sources*. North Mankato, MN: Maupin House Publishing.

Bickford, J. H. (2012). Original political cartoon methodology and adaptations. *Social Studies Research and Practice, 7*(2), 91–101.

Boerman-Cornell, W. (2015). Using historical graphic novels in high school history classes: Potential for contextualization, sourcing, and corroborating. *The History Teacher, 48*(2), 209–224.

Botzakis, S. (2015). Graphic novels in education: Comics, comprehension, and the content areas. In D. Wooten & B. Cullinan (Eds.), *Children's literature in the reading program: Engaging young readers in the 21st century* (96-108). Newark, DE: International Reading Association.

Brozo, W., Moorman, G., & Meyer, C. (2014). *Wham! Teaching with graphic novels across the curriculum*. New York, NY: Teachers College Press.

Bryant, J. (2013). *A splash of red: The life and art of Horace Pippin*. New York, NY: Alfred A. Knopf.

Carano, K. & Clabough, J. (2016). Images of struggle: Teaching human rights with graphic novels. *The Social Studies, 107*(1), 14-18.

Carr, E. (1961). *What is history?* New York, NY: Vintage Books.

Clabough, J., Turner, T., Russell, W., & Waters, S. (2016). *Unpuzzling history with primary sources*. Charlotte, NC: Information Age Publishing.

Clark, J. S. (2014). Teaching historical agency: Explicitly connecting past and present with graphic novels. *Social Studies Research and Practice, 9*(3), 66–80.

Endacott, J. & Brooks, S. (2013). An updated theoretical and practical model for promoting historical empathy. *Social Studies Research and Practice, 8*(1), 41-57.

Engle, S. & Ochoa, A. (1988). *Education for democratic citizenship: Decision making in the social studies*. New York, NY: Teachers College Press.

Giles, C., Wang, Y., Smith, J., & D. Johnson. (2013). "I'm no longer just teaching history." Professional development for teaching Common Core State Standards for literacy in social studies. *Middle School Journal, 44*(3), 34–42.

Helfer, A. (2006). *Malcolm X: A graphic biography*. New York, NY: Hill and Wang.

Helfer, A. (2007). *Ronald Reagan: A graphic biography*. New York, NY: Hill and Wang.

Hennessey, J. (2008). *The United States Constitution: A graphic adaptation*. New York, NY: Hill and Wang.

Jacobson, S. (2006). *The 9/11 Report: A graphic adaptation*. New York, NY: Hill and Wang.

Layne, S. (2015). *In defense of read-aloud: Sustaining best practice*. Portland, ME: Stenhouse Publishers.

Levstik, L. & Barton, K. (2015). *Doing history: Investigating with elementary and middle schools* (5th ed.), New York, NY: Routledge.

Lewis, J. & Aydin, A. (2015). *March book two*. Marietta, GA: Top Shelf Books.

Markel, M. (2013). *Brave girl: Clara and the Shirtwaist Makers' Strike of 1909*. New York, NY: Harper Collins.

NMSA. (2010). *This we believe: Keys to educating young adolescents*. Westerville, OH: Author.

NCSS. (1991). *Social studies in the middle school.* Retrieved from http://www.socialstudies. org/positions/middleschool.

NCSS. (2013). *The college, career, and civic life (C3) framework for social studies state standards: Guidance for enhancing the rigor of K-12 civics, economics, geography, and history.* Retrieved from http://socialstudies.org/c3.

Sheffield, C., Chisholm, J., & Howell, P. (2015). More than superheroes and villains: Graphic novels and multimodal literacy in social studies education. *Social Education, 79*(3), 147-150.

Trelease, J. (2013). *The read-aloud handbook* (7th ed.). New York, NY: Penguin Books.

Vest, K. (2005). *Using primary sources in the classroom: Examining our past, understanding our present, and considering our future.* Huntington Beach, CA: Shell Education.

Waters, S. & Russell, W. (2013). Visual literacy strategies for the social studies classroom. In Lintner, T. (Ed.) *Integrative strategies for the K–12 social studies classroom* (209-233). Charlotte, NC: Information Age Publishing.

Wineburg, S., Martin, D., & Monte-Sano, C. (2012). *Reading like a historian: Teaching literacy in middle and high school history classrooms.* New York, NY: Teachers College Press.

Wooten, D. (2000). *Valued voice: An interdisciplinary approach to teaching and learning.* Newark, DE: International Literacy Association.

06

Social Media, Video, and Podcasts: The Exciting World of Digital Tools

While teaching about the South American country of Suriname, the instructor had his students participating in an ongoing blog dialogue with a few Surinamese nationalists and a group of Peace Corps volunteers who had returned from Suriname. The blogging activity stimulated student interest to a level previously unseen in the classroom, which can be attested to by the following student comment:

> I thought this blogging activity was an excellent way to learn about different cultures because it's from people with firsthand knowledge and who actually lived it, not like a textbook. It's more real when you hear it directly from a person and I think you get more information that way. Plus you can ask questions and know you're getting the correct answer. (Carano, 2006)

In addition, one student said the following about how her stereotypes had changed by participating in the activity:

Before I started reading what you all have posted, I thought of Suriname as a place where there was nothing and didn't have medicine but now I know that you all do and that you are more developed then I have ever imagined…. I had one stereotype and it was a pretty bad one…. When I was told that people lived in the jungle I imagined people like Tarzan and thought that everyone was a crazy jungle people and had tigers for pets…..but now I know that it isn't true there are villages and stores and people have jobs, etc….. sorry about that. (Carano, 2006)

Imagine being able to take your students to another country to learn the subtleties of its culture. In a sense, this is precisely what many social studies teachers are asked to accomplish; technology is one tool that can accomplish this goal by expanding the walls of the traditional classroom (Carano & Stuckart, 2013). As the previous stories suggest, technology allows students to communicate with peers around the globe. AMLE (NMSA,2010) states that middle school students must be empowered to be "successful in a global society." Digital technology provides many exciting tools to enable teachers to lead students down that path.

Learning needs to be relevant to students, and digital technologies can provide this while connecting the classroom to the outside world (Hooft, 2013). The Internet provides increased access to primary sources. This allows teachers to transform mundane learning into more interactive and authentic learning experiences. In this chapter, the focus shifts to the positive role various digital technologies can play in improving the quality of the social studies classroom while aligning with AMLE's *This We Believe: Keys to Educating Young Adolescents* (NMSA, 2010). These include challenging and empowering students in active and relevant instruction. We focus on classroom best practices in social media, podcasts, and digital simulations. All of these technology tools allow students to have authentic learning experiences and construct their understanding about a topic. These types of activities promote students' higher order thinking skills.

Digital Technology Benefits

Combs (2010) found that technology use in social studies middle school classrooms is still restricted. Teachers primarily use technology for test making, accessing background information, and communicating with parents. It is important that technology not be limited to students and teachers merely getting information from Internet searches. Instead, digital technology should enable students to be producers not consumers of information (Hooft, 2013).

Research has suggested that assuming current students are more technologically savvy than past generations is, at least, partially unfounded (Best, Buhay, & McGuire, 2014). Before a teacher embraces technology as a pedagogical tool, she or he must provide students instruction on wise, technological practices (Waring, 2010). Therefore, it is critical that teachers understand and implement best practices for the various technology mediums. There are three preconditions for successful technology integration: curriculum, audience, and visual learning. The technology should not be mistaken for being more than a resource and should enhance the standards and central questions. Teachers must also know their students' aptitude for using this medium. Middle school students, who are not used to employing technology in the classroom, often have a difficult time when they start using a visual medium. This is because they are used to auditory learning. Consequently, teacher scaffolding is necessary. Failing to provide class time to actually teach the technology tool will lead to students struggling with both the new content and technology (Langran & Alibrandi, 2008). The remaining sections of this chapter focus on specific technology tools and their beneficial uses in the middle school social studies classroom. The three technology tools highlighted include social media, podcasts/vodcasts, and digital simulations.

Social Media

The invention of the web browser has facilitated a historic change in global connectedness. A significant consequence has been the online phenomenon of social media sites (Kirkpatrick, 2006), which are Internet sites where people can come together to communicate with one another (Metz, 2006). Social media tools can come in many forms. The most common classroom tools are blogs, video chats, wikis, and Twitter.

Social media sites provide a forum for extending traditional classrooms with an array of benefits that connect to *This We Believe* (NMSA, 2010) tenets by capitalizing on students' personal backgrounds and experiences to further learning. While research suggests that discussions and collaborations are the most common social media classroom strategies (Chen & Bryer, 2012), Holcomb, Beal, and Lee (2011) found social media used wisely enhances curricula by allowing students to engage in real-world problems. Social media sites can also be used to connect classrooms across the globe while humanizing the "other." The "other" refers to a minority group considered to be different from the majority group residing in the mainstream cultural group. These types of websites increase student learning (Krutka & Carano, 2016).

Videoconferencing now provides teachers and students the opportunity to go on field trips without leaving the classroom (Zaino, 2009). Through this social media tool, classrooms are exploring museums while docents take them on tours and educate students about historical relics through a virtual experience. The Smithsonian American Art Museum, Louvre, and the National World War II Museum in New Orleans are just a few examples of the increasing amount of museums offering teachers and students this opportunity.

Twitter provides an instant-messaging outlet used to encourage students to engage in class activities through a variety of activities, such as centering on primary documents or analytical questions and bringing in outside expert perspectives (Krutka & Milton, 2013). Further, Elavsky, Mislan, and Elavsky (2011) found using Twitter to "back channel" an activity allows students to maintain a dialogue or ask questions while it is happening. This has the potential to expand students' understanding of key class concepts.

Social Media Activity: Cultural Exchange

In this activity, students communicate via a social media exchange with peers in another country. Research demonstrates that students who study cultures in this manner are less likely to have misconceptions reinforced and demonstrate a deeper understanding of geography concepts (Carano & Stuckart, 2013). An additional purpose is to find out how an authentic experience can humanize the curriculum. Students analyze their communication and become sensitive to how peers in another country affect their perspectives. Educational websites have been established allowing safe social media for cross-cultural exchanges with international classrooms (See chapter resources in the Additional Ideas Section at the end of the chapter.). Social media activities are often best established as multi-week activities that entail preparation, collaboration time, and reflection. Skype provides a visual component, which allows for unique learning opportunities. This activity uses Skype but can also be done with other types of social media, such as blogs.

The example activity explores the theme "Who am I?" On the first day, the teacher discusses with students the project's goals and the appropriate, culturally sensitive correspondence. The students spend the remainder of the class period being introduced and practicing on the chosen social media medium. During the next class period, they answer some or all of the Kidlink "Who Am I" discussion questions at *http://www.kidlink.org/drupal/node/135*. The homework assignment is to compose a "Who Am I?" person essay based on their answers to the Kidlink questions. In writing the essay, students should keep in mind that an international partner will be their audience. In class, they share their essays with a partner for feedback and revision, keeping in mind their ultimate audience.

The social media cross-cultural correspondence begins the following day as a group session with the teacher facilitating introductions and providing an overview of their local communities. The next day, using their "Who Am I?" personal essay as an introduction, students begin individual social media correspondence with the chosen cultural counterparts. Over the course of several weeks, they engage in a series of sessions with their cultural counterparts (preferably, every other day) that can be done individually or in pairs. It is suggested that pairings are switched at least once during this series. The teacher also needs to provide prompts that will allow the students to use geography concepts in an authentic learning experience to guide the conversations. For example prompts, see Figure 6.1. On the days in between the Skype sessions, the teacher facilitates a classroom reflection on the previous days' Skype interactions.

Figure 6.1 *Example Social Media Prompts*

Theme	Theme Prompt Question Examples
Culture	• What types of meals does your family eat? • How long do you go to school during the day and year? • What do you learn at school? • What holidays do you celebrate? • How do you celebrate holidays?

Movement	• How do you travel to different places (route, drive, fly, walk)? • Does the country export goods to other places? If so, what and where? • Does the country import goods from other places? If so, what and from where? • Why would people leave or move to the country (jobs, family, climate, war)?
Place	• What is it like where you live? • What is the climate like? • What kinds of physical features are there (mountains, rivers, deserts)? • Describe the people who live there (nationalities, traditions, etc.).

Throughout the process, students keep a blog chronicling what they already know and what they are learning about their counterparts' country. Participants should include conversation snippets to support their assertions. Additionally, students from both countries should be encouraged to read each other's blogs and comment and clarify. This activity connects to AMLE's *This We Believe*. In this document, AMLE asserts, "...learning experiences are greatly enhanced when all students have the technology to access rich content, communicate with others, write for authentic audiences, and collaborate with other learners next door or across the globe" (NMSA, 2010, p. 16). Using these best practices, social media has the potential to provide these opportunities when used as a medium in cross-cultural collaboration.

Podcasts/Vodcasts, Digital Sites

Podcasts, vodcasts, and digital audio can assist an array of learning styles such as visual and aural learners (Peters, 2009). Podcasts or vodcasts in social studies can be used in a variety of ways. They can supplement curricular goals. For example, Colonial Williamsburg uses its re-enactors to share information about life in colonial America from figures such as Thomas Jefferson and Patrick Henry to more common citizens such as weavers, bakers, and blacksmiths.

Secondly, podcasts can provide updates for students on current events through daily access to news sites. On the CNN website, teachers and students can watch a ten-minute daily news segment called *CNN Student News*. This news segment is specifically geared to K–12 learners and keeps them abreast of current world events.

Third, podcasts and vodcasts can take students where they otherwise could not go. Students can be taken to different parts of the world through National Geographic and Peace Corps World Wise Schools.

Other forms of digital sites can also make students aware of social studies critical skills. Access to global newspapers allows students to see the news from different perspectives and encourages critical thinking (Carano & Berson, 2007). "Today's Front Pages" *(http://www.newseum.org/todaysfrontpages)* lets students view more than 900 front pages of newspapers around the world. Global newspapers enable students to explore not only how countries and regions report a similar story from different perspectives but also which stories are emphasized across regions and countries. Additionally, many classrooms can download Internet radio broadcasts with software such as Real Player and Windows Media Player (Risinger, 2006). As a result, the Internet provides classrooms the opportunity to listen to broadcasts from around the world. At http://www.broadcast-live.com, students can access televisions and radio stations from more than 100 countries around the globe, with many of the choices in English.

Digital Music Video Activity: History for Music Lovers

Imagine learning about the French Revolution through a videotaped musical parody of Lady Gaga's *Bad Romance* or about Mary, Queen of Scots by listening and watching *Jenny from the Block*. History for Music Lovers *(https://www. youtube.com/playlist?list=PL2B7233B6FE9075EC)*, which features more than 50 world history music video parodies on YouTube, allows teachers to motivate students while teaching critical literacies. These critical literacy skills can be gained by watching and listening to rewritten songs from popular music to teach about a historical figure or period. History for Music Lovers also creates music videos, complete with costumes and plots, to accompany its song parodies.

Watching and listening to videos and combining them with the textbook or other sources provide students opportunities to compare and contrast texts (visually, musically, and lyrically). The following activity fits into a key AMLE characteristic by using varied learning and teaching approaches to explore multiple viewpoints and new ideas. It enables students to understand how music can be used to compare and contrast a textbook's story to determine author bias and demonstrate how the music video's visual representations and lyrics can aid vocabulary development and information processing.

With a few simple steps, students should be able to construct meaning while linking visual and reading skills. While watching the video, they hone their visual observational skills by cataloging the images and identifying concepts that might be unfamiliar (For example, three estates, tennis court, Bastille, and coup d'état). Next, the focus shifts toward students making inferences and stating what they believe the observations mean (see Figure 6.2 for an example).

Figure 6.2 *Visual Analysis Chart*

Visual Observations	Musician is wearing a white wig and black robe while holding a tennis racket. Then a historical visual of men in a government assembly is portrayed. This is followed by the musician swinging the tennis racket and rifles being picked up.
New Concepts	Tennis court.
Student Inference	Tennis court refers to the Third Estate's act of defiance against the privileged classes and the King.
Reason for Inference	Combined with the visuals, the musician was singing the lyrics, "On a tennis court, we swore to a constitution" followed by "Revolution in France."

The teacher should then probe deeper by asking questions that enhance students' summary and analysis skills and provide a deeper understanding of their inferred knowledge of the concepts and story observations. Once the students have a greater understanding of these concepts, the video is watched again and combined with the textbook reading on the French Revolution. At this stage, students are expected to apply the following questions to both the video and the textbook.

- How and why was the message constructed?
- How could different people understand this information differently?
- Whose perspective, values, and ideology are represented?
- Whose perspectives, values, and ideology are missing?

Next, the teacher oversees a classroom discussion with students sharing insights about these questions. The activity concludes with students using the sources to construct an understanding of how the portrayal of the French Revolution in the music video versus the textbook influences people's perceptions of the event. This has the additional benefit of students' gaining skills to analyze for author bias by using the previous questions to compare and contrast the video and textbook.

For an extension activity, students could make their own music videos about a social studies topic. The materials needed for this endeavor include a digital camera and green screen, which could be done by using green cloth or a green poster board on a wall. The following steps are suggested to produce such an activity (Sheffield & Swan, 2012).

1. Students research, analyze, and gather information on theme.

2. Students create a storyboard that organizes the scenes and types of appropriate backdrops.

3. Students write the script.

4. Select appropriate background images.

5. Record the scene in front of a green screen.

6. Once the scene is recorded, import images into a digital filmmaking program.

After completing the video production, students could present and analyze each other's videos for author bias, using the same questions they used to analyze the sources for the French Revolution. This activity again fits into many of AMLE's characteristics through using varied learning approaches to explore multiple viewpoints and new ideas. It enables students to understand how their own use of music can be used to compare and contrast stories to determine author bias.

Digital Simulations

Digital simulations have the potential to foster higher order thinking skills for middle grades students in social studies while engaging those who are often less involved or eager to engage in classroom learning (Devlin-Scherer & Sardone, 2010). In order for simulations to be used in a manner that increases student learning and helps them understand the issue of simulation oversimplification, it is important that teachers provide a structured environment that ties practice to theory (Moore, Beshke, & Bohan, 2014). The following four steps offer best practices for an effective simulation-based lesson.

1. Introduce the purpose of simulation gaming and characteristics of the medium.

2. Play reflectively and attentively; observe and engage in the problem space.

3. Study independent historical evidence on the historical problem spaces.

4. Discuss, debrief, evaluate, and extend.

 ## Digital Simulation Activity

Students can use a digital simulation to be proactive and gain critical decision-making skills. In this activity, they must critically analyze the decision to drop the atomic bomb on the Japanese. The game World War II and the Atomic Bomb 1945 *(http://www.classzone.com/books/north_carolina/act/abomb/index.html)* allows students to take on the role of President Truman as he decides how to end the war with Japan. The simulation lets students learn about the strategies and strengths of Japan and the Allies and meet with advisors on the atomic bomb's development. The simulation culminates with students using President Truman's diary to choose their war options: invasion, negotiate a peace plan, show the bomb's force and demand surrender, or drop the bomb in a surprise attack.

To begin this activity, students spend the first day getting background information by analyzing primary and secondary sources. Initially, they will look at primary sources. The National Security Archive provides documents that key government officials had leading up to making the decision on whether to drop the bomb. These can be accessed at *http://nsarchive.gwu.edu/NSAEBB/NSAEBB162*. Document topics include background on the atomic project, defining targets, alternatives to first use, the Japanese search for Soviet mediation, the Trinity Test, and the first nuclear strikes. Students should be divided into one of the six groups to analyze these primary sources. In each group, they read at least three primary sources under their topic and fill in the chart (see Figure 6.3) after discussing, reconciling, and synthesizing the information with their group members.

Figure 6.3 *Primary Source Worksheet*

Topic:	
Source #1	
Facts:	
Source #2	
Facts:	
Source #3	
Facts:	

After this initial group work, students use the jigsaw method. In this method, they take the information learned in their groups and individually share with other groups. This allows all students to receive background information on each theme. As homework that evening, students are to read a couple of editorials about the dropping of the atomic bomb. The first reading, *Thank God for the Atomic Bomb*, takes a pro position on the dropping of the bomb. Teachers can access the editorial at *http://www.wsj.com/articles/thank-god-for-the-atom-bomb-1438642925*. The second editorial, *Atomic Bomb—Japan Was Ready To Quit*, is against dropping the bomb. This editorial can be accessed at *http://community.seattletimes.nwsource.com/archive/?date=19950723&slug=2132816*.

The teacher begins the activity's second day by facilitating a discussion on the strengths and weaknesses of using a digital simulation. Next, weaknesses using the game to simulate an environment are discussed (for example, oversimplification and a simulated environment's tendency to dehumanize the process). After this initial discussion, the teacher models the simulation by walking through each stage and having the class determine by majority decision the war decision that concludes the simulation. After the teacher-led modeling exercise, students go through the digital simulation on their own and conclude the simulation by writing their war decision in the President's diary, which is the concluding part of the digital simulation.

It is important for the teacher to provide students with a step-by-step guide on how they should write their persuasive argument in the diary. The students have four choices.

1. Continue to bombard, blockade, and invade the Japanese islands.

2. Negotiate a peace plan that is agreed to by Japan and the Allies.

3. Demonstrate the atomic bomb and then demand unconditional surrender.

4. Use the atomic bomb in a surprise attack on Japan.

Students should start by establishing their position. Drawing on the sources students have accessed over the two days, they should then provide three main reasons that would convince a person that their position is correct. Students' reasoning should be supported with examples. In conclusion, students should summarize the most important details of their stand in one or two sentences. For an example of President Truman's diary entry see Figure 6.4.

Figure 6.4 *Presidential Diary Entry*

Student Name: John Doe
Position: Demonstrate the atomic bomb and then demand unconditional surrender

I believe the United States should let Japan know that we have the atomic bomb by showing footage of what it can do and then give Japan three days to agree to an unconditional surrender. There are three reasons the United States should take this position. Each of my positions are drawn from the primary sources on the National Security Archive site provided in class. First, in document 16 (Memorandum from Arthur B. Compton to the Secretary of War, enclosing "Memorandum on 'Political and Social Problems,' from Members of the 'Metallurgical Laboratory' of the University of Chicago", it is clear a U.S. committee on the use of the atomic bomb was concerned about its use on others. The report instead recommended demonstrating the power of the bomb on a barren island. Not only did they believe this would possibly lead to Japan surrendering, but they were concerned that using the bomb would lead to a worldwide nuclear arms race.

A second reason for demonstrating the bomb first comes from document 20 (Minutes of Meeting Held at the White House on Monday, 18 June 1945 at 1530"). According to this document, discussion occurred over offering Japan the preservation of the emperor as a constitutional monarch. If Japan refused, it was suggested that we should tell Japan about the atomic bomb so they would surrender unconditionally before we needed to use it. These discussions suggest that even our government officials thought it was possible to secure unconditional surrender without the use of the bomb. My final example to support my position comes from document 23 (Memorandum from George L. Harrison to Secretary of War, June 28, 1945, Top Secret, enclosing Ralph Bard "Memorandum on the Use of S-1 Bomb"). This document suggests that many scientists who worked on the atomic bomb did not believe the bomb should be used militarily and that the Under Secretary of the U.S. Navy, Ralph Bard, believed a warning demonstration of the bomb would work to secure surrender and allow the United States to continue to be seen as a humanitarian country.

On the concluding day of the lesson, students participate in a four-corner activity. In this activity, a sign for one of the four war decisions on the simulation should be in the corner of the classroom. Students will go to the corner that has the sign in which they supported during the digital simulation. Using supporting information from the documents they have analyzed over the previous three days, the groups then participate in a debate that defends their group's position. The teacher moderates the debate and explains the expectations. See the list of example debate expectations.

- Be polite and courteous.
- Listen attentively.
- Be respectful and supportive of peers.
- Avoid inappropriate noises.
- Speak only when recognized by the moderator.
- Allow others to express their opinions; do not monopolize the debate.
- Use grammatically correct language.
- Speak clearly, slowly, and loud enough to be heard by the audience.
- Speak with passion and excitement.

Each group is allowed an opening and closing statement. In between, there is time for using sources to provide information that supports the validity of their position.

As the activity demonstrates, digital simulation games allow participants to grapple with weighty issues and provide an opportunity to engage in experiences in a recreated environment. This allows authentic situations while interacting with content, and the activity is pedagogically mediated by the instructor (Wright-Maley, 2015). Students can see through this simulation that people's decisions can have a lasting impact on others.

Conclusion

In *This We Believe* (NMSA, 2010), the point is made that middle school educators should understand the dynamics of an ever-changing youth culture. More than 90% of teens use the Internet (Madden et al., 2013), making teacher understanding of this medium essential. With the exciting potential digital technology has to offer, middle school students can break down the barriers of isolation and collaborate with broad networks of peers, experts, and materials locally, nationally, and globally. The best practices outlined in this chapter can empower educators to tap into the vast array of opportunities that digital technology offers in the middle grades classroom.

Additional Resources

Edmodo *(www.edmodo.com)*: This is a free social networking platform that has been referred to as the Facebook for schools. It is a safe and teacher-controlled environment in which students must be provided an access code to join, and anonymous posting is not possible. Edmodo is primarily a tool for in-class communication, but it also provides several ways for classrooms to connect with other classrooms. There are many features and ways to use Edmodo. A few classroom examples include sharing files and resources with students and other classrooms in real time, creating polls for students to vote online, writing short summaries of lessons for absent student, and posting homework information. Ultimately, a key benefit of Edmodo is that it provides students a safe educational setting to practice the digital-age social networking and learning skills needed in their increasingly connected personal, academic, and future professional lives.

ePALS Classroom Exchange *(www.epals.com)*: Connecting more than 108,000 classrooms in more than 190 countries with school-safe e-mail, ePALS markets itself as the Internet's largest global education community of collaborative classrooms engaged in cross-cultural exchanges and project sharing. Students across cultures can work together on projects that provide benefits such as language acquisition, understanding cultural nuances, and literary exchanges.

Peace Corps World Wise Schools *(www.peacecorps.gov/wws)*: This site provides classroom resources and lesson plans based on the experiences of Peace Corps volunteers around the world. Teachers can use the website to establish a classroom match with Peace Corps volunteers currently serving overseas in Central/South America, Africa, and Asia/Eastern Europe. A middle school classroom can have its own personal cultural correspondent living overseas with the Peace Corps volunteer. Additionally, the website enables teachers to connect with returned Peace Corps volunteers in the local community as guest speakers. Opportunities, such as these, provide students authentic learning experiences and exposure to realia, which are objects and materials from a cultural group's everyday life in geographic areas they may be studying in the classroom.

International Education and Resource Network (iEARN) *(www.iearn.org)*: This site is a nonprofit global network made up of more than 30,000 schools in more than 140 countries. Teachers and students collaborate via the Internet on projects that fit their curricula and increase international understanding. Middle school teachers can use this network to engage students in service-learning projects around the globe. Example projects middle school students have worked on include intercultural murals, improving education opportunities for females around the world, and sustainable development. By working via social media with students across the globe on these projects, students are able to learn to collaborate across cultures while working on making positive change in others' lives.

#sschat: An ongoing Twitter *(www.twitter.com)* discussion that serves as informal professional development for social studies educators by allowing participants to join to discuss and learn about current social studies teaching trends, how to integrate technology, transform their teaching, and connect with inspiring social studies educators world-wide. One hour long moderated topical chats are held at 7 p.m. (EST) each Monday. Each chat revolves around a different topic that social studies teachers are using in the classroom. Example topics include teaching with primary sources, teaching history with video, and assessment in social studies. An archived list of the chats can be found at sschat.org.

Museum Box *(museumbox.e2bn.org):* A great tool for creating virtual displays of artifacts that you find online. By using Museum Box, students can organize images, texts, videos, links, and audio clips about any topic that they are researching. When completed, students' "boxes" become digital dioramas. The website provides the tools for teachers and students to build up an argument or description of an event, person, or historical period by placing items in a virtual box.

Library of Congress *(www.loc.gov/teachers/tps):* Teachers can sign up for the TPS (Teaching with Primary Sources) journal. There are also internal links to music, poetry, and lessons with Library of Congress resources. Middle school social studies teachers can use this site to access thousands of primary sources, which they can use to supplement lessons. Access to such a wealth of primary sources provides students a window into the daily lives of individuals living in the past. Additionally, by reading and analyzing primary sources, students are able to arrive at their own conclusions based on their understanding of the documents.

Crash Course *(www.youtube.com/user/crashcourse)* John Green does a series of short YouTube educational videos known as Crash Course that outline major events in U.S. history in a fun and amusing way. The videos were created to make history relatable and manageable for a generation of students who digest digital media on a daily basis. John Green summarizes events in history, including social, political, economic, and cultural history. Teachers can use the videos as an overview to spark critical thinking and discussion in class. Students can connect with various elements embedded in the medium. Some students may enjoy the thought bubble, cartoon video portions, or perhaps the primary source mystery document.

References

Best, L. A., Buhay, D. N., & McGuire, K. P. (2014). The millennial student: Implications for technology in education. *Meridian Middle School Computer Technologies Journal, 17,* article 2.

Carano, K. (2006, May 14). *Suriname.* Retrieved from http://caranok.edublogs.org.

Carano, K. T. & Berson, M. J. (2007). Breaking stereotypes: Constructing geographic literacy and cultural awareness through technology. *The Social Studies, 98*(2), 65-70.

Carano, K. T. & Stuckart, D. W. (2013). Blogging for global literacy and cross-cultural awareness. In L. Nganga, J. Kambutu, & W. B. Russell III (Eds.), *Exploring globalization opportunities and challenges in social studies: Effective instructional approaches* (pp. 179-196). New York, NY: Peter Lang.

Chen, B. & Bryer, T. (2012). Investigating instructional strategies for using social media in formal and informal learning. *The International Review of Research in Open and Distance Learning, 13*(1), 87-100.

Combs, H. J. (2010). Instructional technology: Status in middle and high school social studies. *National Teacher Education Journal, 3*(3), 23-31.

Devlin-Scherer, R. & Sardone, N. B. (2010). Digital simulation games for social studies classrooms. *The Clearing House, 83,* 138-144.

Elavsky, C. M, Mislan, C., & Elavsky, S. (2011). When talking less is more. Exploring outcomes of Twitter usage in the large-lecture hall. *Learning, Media, and Technology, 36*(3), 215-233.

Holcomb, L., Beal, C., & Lee, J. K. (2011). Supersizing social studies through the use of Web 2.0 technologies. *Social Studies Research and Practice, 6*(3), 102-111.

Hooft, M. V. (2013). Taking it to the street: Using QR codes to tell student-created (hi) stories on location. *Social Education. 77*(2), 99-101.

Kirkpatrick, D. (2006). Life in a connected world. *Fortune, 154*(1), 98–100.

Krutka, D. G. & Carano, K. T. (2016). "As long as I see you on Facebook I know you are safe": Social media experiences as humanizing pedagogy. In A. Crowe & A. Cuenca (Eds.), *Rethinking social studies education in the twenty-first century* (207-222). New York, NY: Springer International Publishing.

Krutka, D. & Milton, M. K. (2013). The enlightenment meets twitter: Using social media in the social studies classroom. *Ohio Social Studies Review, 50*(2), 22-29.

Langran, E. & Alibrandi, M. (2008). Middle school social studies teachers integration of technology to meet 21st century challenges. *Meridian Middle School Computer Technologies Journal, 11*(2), article 4.

Madden, M., Lenhart, A. Duggan, M, Cortesi, S., & Gasser, U. (2013). *Teens and Technology 2013.* Washington, D.C.: Pew Internet & American Life Project.

Metz, C. (2006). MySpace nation. *PC Magazine, 25*(12), 76–80, 83–84, 87.

Moore, C., Beshke, C., & Bohan, C. (2014). Simulations and games in the civics classroom. *Social Studies and Research Practice, 9*(2), 77-88.

NMSA. (2010). *This we believe: Keys to educating young adolescents.* Westerville, OH: Author.

Peters, L. (2009). *Global education. Using technology to bring the world to your students.* Eugene, OR: ISTE

Risinger, C. F. (2006). Teaching about international issues, geography, and multiple points of view using the Internet. *Social Education, 70*(1), 34–36.

Sheffield, C. C. & Swan, S. B. (2012). Digital reenactments: Using green screen technology to recreate the past. *Social Education, 76*(2), 92-95.

Waring, S. M. (2010). The impact of a technology coordinator's belief system upon using technology to create a community's history. *Computers in the Schools, 27,* 76-98.

Wright-Maley, C. (2015). On "stepping back and letting go": The role of control in the success or failure of social studies simulations. *Theory & Research in Social Education, 43*(2), 206-243.

Zaino, J. (2009). Field-tripping goes virtual. *Instructor, 119*(2), 34-36.

07

Writing to Think:
Thinking to Write

A vital component of any middle school social studies curriculum is an emphasis on writing. Writing is a means by which students can capture and then revise their thoughts (Robb, 2010). The National Council for Teachers of English (NCTE) stresses that writing allows students to generate ideas and communicate their understanding of those ideas (NCTE, 2016). The steps of writing are intrinsic to the overall goals of social studies as envisioned by the National Council of the Social Studies (NCSS). NCSS emphasizes that students must possess discipline-based literacy skills to critically explore topics in depth (NCSS, 2016).

In this chapter, we explore the role that writing can play in the middle school social studies classroom. We begin by discussing the importance of writing to the C3 Framework. The chapter shifts to briefly focus on key reasons why children struggle to write, and we provide recommendations to address these. We then give some of the purposes for writing. The remaining sections of the chapter contain classroom activities that highlight these reasons for writing. An appendix is included with additional writing activities connected to these same purposes for writing.

The Importance of Writing with Current Educational Reform Movements

Writing is a vital component of the C3 Framework by NCSS. It stresses that students should analyze texts and communicate their understanding by summarizing key content material, articulating the biases and perspectives within a text, drawing conclusions with evidence, and creating solutions to historical and contemporary problems (NCSS, 2013a). Students use writing activities to capture and demonstrate their mastery of analysis skills when reading a text (Clabough, Turner, Russell, & Waters, 2016). We argue that writing activities are key assessments to be used by students to meet expectations of all social studies standards.

Reasons that Students Struggle as Writers

As Andy Griffith's television character Ben Matlock was fond of saying, "Ain't nothing easy." Matlock's catch phrase is applicable when trying to teach students to be successful writers. Middle school students constantly struggle with writing. There are many reasons that students struggle with writing. Space only allows us to mention two of these reasons. First, students may have not received sufficient scaffolding. If writing has not been consistently taught in the early grades, students have had insufficient practice and help. This creates a writing deficit (NCTE, 2016). A large percentage of our students enter our middle school classrooms with only a fragmented understanding and limited awareness of how to write.

Second, students have not developed a motivation to write. They see little relevancy of the writing assignments to their daily lives. Another factor in motivation to writing is students' lack of choices and power in writing assignments. The writing assignments given to them tend to be boring, lackluster, and purposeless. All of these items taken together create a perfect storm for the teacher to feel like she is pulling teeth to get the students to complete writing assignments.

Solving the Problem

Teachers can mediate students' writing problems with carefully planned scaffold techniques (NCTE, 2014). It is important to remember that every student will be at a different point in writing fluency. Therefore, the scaffolding needed will likely vary from class to class and even from student to student. Writing is a building process (Wooten, 2000). It simultaneously builds several sub-skills and then fits them together in each single writing product. The teacher has to help students with multiple steps in this process. She needs to evaluate where her students are in the writing process and then provide remediation based on the areas of difficulty.

Good writing requires more than skill. There is a substantial emotional component connected to students' desire to write and their belief that they have something to say. Teachers need to begin with short writing assignments to build student confidence. For example, the teacher may ask students to write a historical tweet from the perspective of John Adams about the role of the federal government. A historical tweet is simply students writing in the role of a historical figure using the technology medium of Twitter, which many of them use in their daily lives (Turner, Clabough, & Cole, 2013). After students complete their short writing assignments, the teacher can talk about the language used with tweets and discuss how this type of writing does not reflect grammar used in daily communications in a professional setting. This helps the teacher discuss the concept of code switching with students when writing for different audiences. The teacher should model examples of different writing activities and gradually build the length and complexity of such assignments, which strengthens students' writing skills.

One way the teacher can actively engage students in writing assignments is to allow them choices (Robb, 2010). For example, students may write a short correspondence between Abraham Lincoln and Jefferson Davis. Several other short assignments with this same time period may include letters to President Lincoln or his cabinet, telegrams in context to General McLellan, or letters home as soldiers on the Union or Confederacy side. It is important that we sometimes give choices with writing assignments about a historical topic. This allows students to take more ownership of their own learning.

Another way to encourage student interest is through the introduction of strong mentor texts. Mentor texts refer to class readings that can serve as strong models of quality writing and also contain social studies content material. Students need to read good writing in order to be good writers (Alber, 2014). Some examples include Lincoln's *Gettysburg Address*, Dr. King's *I Have a Dream*, Sojourner Truth's *Ain't I Woman*, and Winston Churchill's *Iron Curtain*. Students can explore the contents, words, and phrases within mentor texts to see examples of quality writing and then replicate the same approaches in their own writings. For example, they may examine the good components within a mentor text such as the words, phrases, and ideas used by FDR during one of his Fireside Chats.

Mentor texts enable students to deconstruct the strong components within a piece of writing (Alber, 2014). By this, we mean that students are able to identify the factors that make the writing great. These readings also provoke interest in the material, can lead to more in-depth discussions about a topic, and capture the essence about certain aspects with the material (Pytash & Morgan, 2014). The four writing activities discussed later in this chapter contain mentor texts (Additional types of reading materials that can serve as mentor texts are provided in chapter five.).

Writing for Different Purposes

It is important for students to realize that people write for different purposes. This means that students' writing needs to be done with a clear purpose in mind. Here are some examples.

- Summarizing events, arguments, ideas, facts, and written and oral presentations.

- Convincing others of one's beliefs, logic, relevancy, and preponderance of evidence.

- Criticizing or praising the work, accomplishments, or ideas of others.

- Telling a story that may or may not be to make a point.

- Describing an experience or something seen or heard.

- Interpreting something said or written by others.

- Making explanations.

- Comparing and/or contrasting two different things, people, or sets of ideas.

- Consolidating and coordinating a number of sources.

- Solving problems (Clabough, Turner, Russell, & Waters, 2016).

This list of purposes for writing is far from exhaustive, but it does connect to many of the analysis skills stressed within the C3 Framework. Teachers need to use writing activities that enable students to employ these analysis skills in their responses (Monte-Sano, 2012). These types of writing activities reflect the best intentions of classroom activities and assessments as discussed in AMLE's *This We Believe* (NMSA, 2010). In the remaining sections of this chapter, we provide writing activities that connect to the purposes of writing discussed in the list above.

ACTIVITY

Summarizing Academic Vocabulary in Social Studies

It is almost universally recognized that students must grasp many terms in order to successfully navigate and understand any social studies unit of study. We call these set terms "academic language" (Marzano & Pickering, 2005). The teacher needs to provide texts that allow students to see academic language utilized numerous times in meaningful ways. This writing activity is aimed at helping students use evidence from a graphic novel to explain a key term.

Students will examine *March Book One* (Lewis & Aydin, 2013), which focuses on issues that brought John Lewis to the Civil Rights Movement along with some events of the movement. This graphic novel is an ideal text to help students learn the term *non-violent civic disobedience*. Grasping this term helps students gain an understanding of approaches used by many civil rights activists during the 1950s and 1960s.

The teacher starts by providing examples of non-violent civic disobedience from this graphic novel. The students should fill in part of the word web as the teacher demonstrates an example with this term. The teacher then breaks the students into groups to complete the graphic organizer using examples of this term in *March Book One*. Based on students' word web, it is hoped that their understanding of non-violent civic disobedience will be strengthened and clarified.

After students complete the word web in groups, the teacher facilitates a class debriefing by asking students to elaborate on their answers and clarify any misconceptions they have about this term. The debriefing needs to be followed by students writing a paragraph explaining their view of non-violent civic disobedience with evidence from their graphic organizer and class discussion. See Figure 7.1 for an example of a word web written by a sixth grade student.

Figure 7.1 *Student Word Web for One Version of Pope Urban II's Speech*

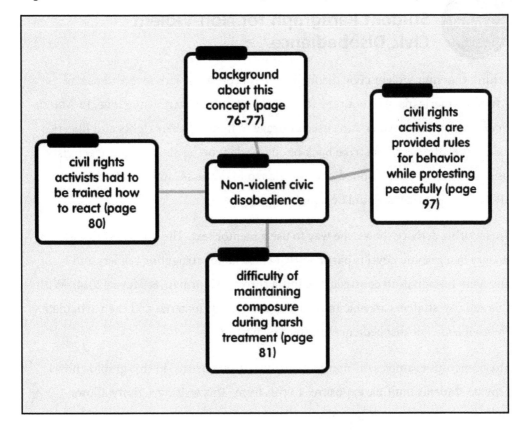

Student Paragraph for Non-Violent Civic Disobedience

I think that non-violent civic disobedience is protesting with love and peace. African Americans used courage to fight for what they want using love. In *March Book One*, African Americans used courage to fight for their rights and liberties using love. They did not strike back or curse when being abused. These activists used nonviolent civic disobedience similar to Mahatma Gandhi so that one day all American citizens would be equal.

This writing activity shows one way to use a mentor text. The use of words and images in a graphic novel is particularly beneficial for struggling readers and emergent bilinguals to construct meaning (Brozo, Moorman, & Meyer, 2014). With this activity, students are able to read and summarize material and then articulate "non-violent civic disobedience" in their own words.

The numerous examples of "non-violent civic disobedience" in this graphic novel provide students multiple exposures to this term. This writing activity allows students to "hypothesize, organize information into useful and meaningful constructs…" (NMSA, 2010, p.16). It is the examination of historical terms in this level of depth that leads to student comprehension.

Helping Students Contextualize the Past

People's actions and events of history unfold within the social, cultural, political, and economical backdrop of a time period. Contextualizing issues, actions, and events in a society allow students to see how historical figures cajole, persuade, inspire, and manipulate others to support their ideas and plans; in other words, students see how history is made (Levstik & Barton, 2015). One set of reading materials that can be used to accomplish this goal is historical fiction.

Good historical fiction conveys the essence of an individual from a time period or contextualizes life in a society. Such writing can help students understand some aspects of the social and cultural feelings in a time period. This is due to the fact that accurate details in every day activities in a society are included. For example, *An Elephant in the Garden* (Morpurgo, 2013) captures the desperation that people felt fleeing the bombing of Dresden at the end of World War II. In flashbacks, the reader also sees the divide among the German people about the Nazi regime. Good historical fiction helps students better understand previous time periods and the people that influenced societies.

The activity to help students contextualize a time period is a perspective-writing piece in the form of a letter. We will use *Breaking Stalin's Nose* (Yelchin, 2013) as an example to show the power that good historical fiction can have in teaching. This book focuses on Sasha and his dream to become a Young Pioneer in the Soviet Union. However, Sasha's life is soon turned upside down when his father, a member of the secret police, is arrested in the middle of the night. Sasha goes to school the next day homeless and accidently breaks the nose of a bust of Stalin. The school actively seeks to find the perpetrator of this act. Throughout this ordeal, Sasha begins to question his beliefs about Soviet society and the role that Joseph Stalin has played in shaping the world around him.

Students read the short chapters in this book in groups of four. They should take notes about the harsh conditions along with the unhealthy social and cultural climate in the Soviet Union. While not technically making an appearance in this book, Stalin makes his presence felt throughout the book. Students need to take notes and discuss the contents of this book in their groups. After completing a couple of chapters, the teacher should bring the class back together for a class debrief. Students will want to add to their notes comments from peers.

The steps described above need to continue until the groups finish reading *Breaking Stalin's Nose*. This will take more than one class period. The teacher should provide students with instructions for a perspective-writing activity. Assume the role of Sasha and write a letter to the United Nations asking for help against Stalin's oppressive regime. Students will want to use their notes to discuss examples that show the oppression in Soviet society. We have provided an example letter below.

Example of Sasha's Letter to the United Nations

To Whom It May Concern,

I am writing this letter hoping that it reaches the United Nations. All of the people in the Soviet Union need help. Comrade Stalin has made life unbearable for all of us in the Soviet Union. It took me some time to realize this. My father was arrested for no reason except that one of my neighbors wanted to move into the apartment that my father and I shared. I tried to ask for help from my aunt, but she would not take me in out of fear. This is life on a daily basis in the Soviet Union.

After my father was arrested, I went to school the next day homeless where I accidently broke the nose of a bust of Comrade Stalin. The school went into chaos when this was discovered. You would have thought that top secrets at the highest level of government had been stolen. The principal and teachers interrogated the students to determine the culprit of this deed. I thought school was supposed to be a place of learning? This climate is the type of fear and paranoia common in Soviet society. Comrade Stalin has turned us against each other to the point where everyone is guilty of treason against the state.

I ask for your help because I see no way for the Soviet people to solve our own problems. This is no way for anyone to live. If you receive this letter, chances are that it will be too late to help me. I will probably be one of the many faces in my school photos that have been blackened out. Perhaps, your actions can make a difference for another child in my beloved Soviet Union.

Sasha

This writing activity gives students the opportunity to explore an alternative plan of action that Sasha never had. It also helps students conceptualize the paranoia and fear rampant in Soviet society during Stalin's reign. They can also see the human toll that the oppression of the Stalin regime had on people in Soviet society. Good historical fiction transports students into a time period. Learning about history in the manner discussed in this activity leaves an imprint in students' minds about the issues and events of a social studies curriculum (NMSA, 2010).

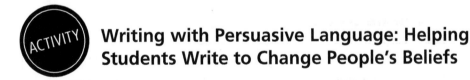

Writing with Persuasive Language: Helping Students Write to Change People's Beliefs

On a daily basis, students are exposed to people trying to convince them to buy or believe in different products and ideas. These encounters range from sources such as the Internet, television, friends, and family. More and more sources attempting to influence the way they think or act are encountered in adulthood. Politicians, sales representatives, car dealers, and bosses are just a few of these. Students themselves must often use persuasive language. These realities are compelling reasons for middle school social studies teachers to help students examine not only the nature of persuasive language but also how to effectively communicate with persuasive language (Austin & Thompson, 2015).

One way teachers can have students explore the nature of persuasive language is to have students construct a writing example. For the purposes of this activity, we focus on writing a persuasive piece on why George Custer should be in the "U.S. Generals' Hall of Fame." The teacher should obtain multiple sources about General Custer from a combination of websites and books and put excerpts from these readings at different learning stations. Some of the topics at the stations may include Custer's military record during the U.S. Civil War at Gettysburg and Appomattox and his shortcomings at the Battle of Little Big Horn. Students' exploration of the material at the stations will help them build an argument for Custer entering the "U.S. Generals' Hall of Fame." Each group is responsible for one of three tasks at the stations: constructing a timeline of Custer's life, making a list of his successes and accomplishments, and collecting testimonials from his admirers. The reading material at each station needs to contain different information about George Custer's accomplishments and shortcomings. See Figure 7.2 for a table of resources about Custer for use in the stations.

Figure 7.2 *Websites and Books for George Custer*

Websites for General Custer	http://www.biography.com/people/george-custer-9264128
	http://www.civilwar.org/education/history/biographies/george-armstrong-custer-1.html
	http://www.pbs.org/weta/thewest/people/a_c/custer.htm
	http://www.history.com/topics/george-armstrong-custer
	https://www.gilderlehrman.org/history-by-era/development-west/timeline-terms/george-armstrong-custer

Books for General Custer	McMurtry, L. (2012). *Custer.* New York, NY: Simon & Schuster.
	Edge, D.(2015). *Custer's trials: A life on the frontier of a new America.* New York, NY: Alfred Knopf.
	Robbins, J. (2014). *The real Custer: From boy general to tragic hero.* New York, NY: Perseus Distribution.

In groups of four, students rotate to each of the stations and take notes about George Custer. They should discuss what each source in the stations adds to their knowledge about him. The teacher needs to float around to help students with their research at the stations. After students have rotated to each station, they share their findings in a teacher-guided debriefing.

After the debriefing, the teacher provides a prompt for the students to individually create a persuasive writing piece: "Assume the role of General Custer and write a brief memo on why you should be included in the 'U.S. Generals' Hall of Fame.'" The students need to use evidence collected from reviewing the sources at the stations along with the class debrief to write their persuasive piece. It is recommended that the teacher provide a sample persuasive piece to model the elements used to make persuasive arguments. Below is an example of a student's persuasive writing piece.

Example Memo for General Custer's Pitch to Be in the "U.S. Generals' Hall of Fame"

I want to make this august body aware of my accomplishments and qualifications. Once you understand these, there is no doubt that you will want to include me in the "U.S. Generals' Hall of Fame." Sure, things at the Battle of Little Big Horn did not go my way, but a general's career is not defined by one event. Even the great Washington, who is revered by all of us, lost a lot of battles before realizing that shooting at people standing in straight lines from behind trees is a good idea. I demonstrated a keen insight into military strategy with the First Battle of Bull Run and the Battle of Gettysburg. My bold strategies in my cavalry regiment helped me to constantly be promoted. My detractors can call me the "Boy General" all they want; they are just envious of my success. Sure, I lost at Little Big Horn but need I remind you that General Lee also lost the U.S. Civil War thanks to me cutting off the movement of his forces at Appomattox. That is right I played an instrumental part in helping end the bloody conflict that cost many Americans' lives. I ask for these reasons and many more that the committee carefully consider my application into the "U.S. Generals' Hall of Fame." My absence from this esteemed group is a miscarriage of justice that is a glaring omission and an insult to my many accomplishments.

Colonel (Former General) George Armstrong Custer

The students need to edit their persuasive pieces before sharing with the class. The teacher should ask students to highlight the reasons that they used certain pieces of evidence and language to make their persuasive argument. This provides students with experience recognizing language and examples of persuasive arguments in written documents and public speeches. It is important for students to decode persuasive language used in an argument in order to make informed decisions (Ochoa-Becker, 2007). This writing activity also gives students practice making arguments through the use of evidence, which is a key component to successfully meeting the standards in the C3 Framework (Giles, Wang, Smith, & Johnson, 2013). This short memo activity enables students to make persuasive arguments, which will help them to be successful throughout their academic and professional careers (NMSA, 2010).

Problem Solving with the "Fantastic Four" in the "Age of Jackson"

ACTIVITY

With a democracy, people disagree—a lot. John Adams had to break the most ties as Vice President in the U.S. Senate during the First Congress. The interaction of people from regions of the U.S. with different cultural, social, political, and religious beliefs shaping public policies often creates conflicting ideas. This does not even take into account when countries with different interests interact with each other.

Students need to be able to examine differing, and often conflicting, views about a historical event and offer solutions to an issue. This enables them to understand how values impact people's actions. In this activity, we turn to the example of American politics in the 1820s and 1830s. The period was heavily influenced by "The Fantastic Four": Andrew Jackson, Henry Clay, Daniel Webster, and John C. Calhoun. Students should scrutinize key historical figures' views on issues such as the role of the federal government, foreign policy, secession, nullification, and the Second Bank of the United States. The teacher should provide students with some primary sources and/or excerpts from books that capture these historical figures' perspectives on an issue. After students have spent some time doing this, they can write in the role of one of the "Fantastic Four." This activity prepares students for forming opinions and making decisions in their own world (NCSS, 2013b).

For this activity, students are split into groups to research these four individuals' stances on an issue provided by the teacher. The teacher may ask students to discuss the issue with the role of the federal government from these four gentlemen's perspective. Each member of the group should assume the responsibility of researching the opinion on the role of the federal government from one member of the "Fantastic Four" and then report his or her findings to the other group members. Each group then selects the one historical figure that they agree with on this issue. The groups need to capture their evidence about the four historical figures.

After the students research and discuss their findings with group members, they share their findings with the class. The teacher should guide the discussion and ask groups to elaborate on their points. Students need to fill in the graphic organizer while listening to peers. This class discussion allows students to learn from their peers and enables the teacher to clarify any questions. At the end of this class discussion, the groups write a short piece from the perspective of their selected historical figure. The students should work collaboratively to write and edit this piece. See the following example of how Henry Clay would view the role of the federal government.

Example of Henry Clay Perspective Writing Piece

We are the inheritors of a great nation. Our fathers laid the foundation with ideas for this country to flourish. It is our responsibility and duty to put into place the mechanisms to allow our people to flourish. As we spread the ideals of liberty and justice across this great land, our people need their government to take steps that make this process easier. For starters, our government should be in the business of constructing high-quality roads to make transportation easier. Good roads will allow our people easier transportation and permit the movement of goods. This, in turn, will stimulate our economy and bind us together as one nation. There is a moral imperative owed by this nation to support the people of this great nation.

This activity allows students to analyze evidence about an issue from four distinct perspectives and then articulate the positions that they favor. Through all of these processes, students strengthen their problem-solving skills with the use of evidence to support their arguments (Engle, 1960). They also demonstrate their understanding about an issue from the perspective of an historical figure. This helps student gain a deeper understanding of an individual by articulating his or her values and beliefs in their writing pieces (Austin & Thompson, 2015) and prepares students to be problem solvers in their life choices (NMSA, 2010).

Conclusion

The function and importance of writing in our social studies classrooms have dramatically increased with the advent of the C3 Framework. Writing is a quintessential vehicle by which students communicate their understanding and analysis of the content contained in reading materials. The examination of powerful mentor texts and completion of writing activities to articulate and capture their ideas about class readings provide opportunities for students to explore social studies content material in more depth. This chapter provides only a few examples of the ways that social studies teachers can integrate writing activities into their middle school classrooms. The skills gained by reading mentor texts and constructing writing assignments help prepare students to thrive and succeed in an information-driven society in the 21st century (NCSS, 2016; NMSA, 2010).

Additional Writing Activities

1. The teacher can have students explore differences of opinion among different historical figures through letter writing activities. For example, Thomas Jefferson and John Adams carried on a personal correspondence after their presidencies about a range of issues. Students can review these letters and then assume the role of one former president. They can then respond as Jefferson or Adams to an existing letter. This allows students to see how people have different beliefs about issues in a time period as well as the reasons for these differences in personal philosophy.

2. Students can use writing activities to become storytellers. They can assume the role of a historical figure and write a story connected to an event. For example, they could research the Boston Tea Party and then use these facts to write a story as a participant in this event. After writing and editing, these stories can be shared. This activity enables students to see how people shape the interpretation and significance of historical events through the transmission of personal stories.

3. Our students need to practice summarizing academic vocabulary in social

studies curricula. One way this can be accomplished is by students creating storyboards to represent these vocabulary terms. Storyboards allow students to use words, images, facial expressions, and thought bubbles to convey a chronological narrative about an item. For example, students could create a storyboard to show how the Irish Potato Famine connects to push/pull factors with human migration. Push/pull factors refer to items that cause people to migrate to and away from cities, states, and even countries. This activity enables students to communicate their understanding of important social studies academic vocabulary.

4. Students need to be able to use multiple sources together to formulate their arguments. One way this can be accomplished is by giving multiple sources about a topic and asking students to use those texts as the basis to form an argument about a topic. For example, students may examine multiple documents about the "divine right of kings" and then write a brief summary using these sources to explain this concept. This gives students experience with using evidence to formulate their arguments.

5. There are many things in our curriculum that students must compare and contrast. One key item is the difference of opinion about issues and ideas in society. The conflict between Galileo and the Catholic Church can serve as a great example for examining differences in opinion. Students may read primary sources and create a twitter war between Pope Paul V and Galileo. The goal of the texts created by students is to capture the differences of opinions between these two men. This activity allows students to see how people form their arguments as well as the influences that impact our choices, decisions, and beliefs.

References

Alber, R. (2014). Using mentor texts to motivate and support student writing. *Edutopia*. Retrieved from http://www.edutopia.org/blog/using-mentor-text-motivate-and-support-student-writers-rebecca-alber.

Austin, H. & Thompson, K. (2015). *Examining the evidence: Seven strategies for teaching with primary sources*. North Mankato, MN: Maupin House Publishing.

Brozo, W., Moorman, G., & Meyer, C. (2014). *Wham! Teaching with graphic novels across the curriculum*. New York, NY: Teachers College Press.

Clabough, J., Turner, T., Russell, W., & Waters, S. (2016). *Unpuzzling history with primary sources.* Charlotte, NC: Information Age Publishing.

Engle, S. (1960). Decision making: The heart of the social studies. *Social Education, 24*(7), 301–306.

Giles, C., Wang, Y., Smith, J., & D. Johnson. (2013). "I'm no longer just teaching history." Professional development for teaching Common Core State Standards for literacy in social studies. *Middle School Journal, 44*(3), 34–42.

Levstik, L. & Barton, K. (2015). *Doing history: Investigating with elementary and middle schools* (5th ed.), New York, NY: Routledge.

Lewis, J. & Aydin, A. (2013). *March book one.* Marietta, GA: Top Shelf Productions.

Marzano, R. & Pickering, D. (2005). *Building academic vocabulary: Teacher's manual.* Alexandria, VA: Association for Supervision & Curriculum Development.

Monte-Sano, C. (2012). Build skills by doing history. *Phi Delta Kappan, 94*(3), 62-65.

Morpurgo, M. (2013). *An elephant in the garden.* New York, NY: Square Fish.

NCSS. (2013a). *The college, career, and civic life (C3) framework for social studies state standards: Guidance for enhancing the rigor of K-12 civics, economics, geography, and history.* Retrieved from http://socialstudies.org/c3.

NCSS. (2013b). *Revitalizing civic learning in our schools.* Retrieved from http://www. socialstudies.org/positions/revitalizing_civic_learning.

NCSS. (2016). A vision of powerful teaching and learning in social studies. *Social Education, 80*(3), 180-182.

National Council of Teachers of English [NCTE]. (2014). *NCTE beliefs about students' right to write.* Retrieved from http://www.ncte.org/positions/statements/students-right-to-write.

NCTE. (2016). *Professional knowledge for the teaching of writing.* Retrieved from http://www.ncte.org/positions/statements/teaching-writing.

NMSA. (2010). (2010). *This we believe: Keys to educating young adolescents.* Westerville, OH: Author.

Ochoa-Becker, A. (2007). *Democratic education for social studies: An issues-centered decision making curriculum.* Charlotte, NC: Information Age Publishing.

Pytash, K. & Morgan, D. (2014). Using mentor texts to teach writing in science and social studies. *The Reading Teacher, 68*(2), 93-102.

Robb, L. (2010). *Teaching middle school writers: What every English teacher needs to know.* Portsmouth, NH: Heinemann.

Turner, T., Clabough J., & Cole, W. (2013). An "urgent brief": Social studies and writing skills. *Middle Level Learning, 47,* 13-16.

Wooten, D. (2000). *Valued voice: An interdisciplinary approach to teaching and learning.* Newark, DE: International Literacy Association.

Yelchin, E. (2013). *Breaking Stalin's nose.* New York, NY: Square Fish.

08

From Stage Fright to Drama Queens: Ham on Wry

In their dreams, most middle schoolers want to be heroes, stars, and popular kids. They are drama queens—the girls, the guys, even the shy ones. They go from angst to elation to ennui to rebellious anger in seconds. Drama is their thing. However, there are also inhibitions that are most active during the middle years—shyness, need for peer acceptance, and desire to succeed. The great thing is that drama helps them get through their range of emotions.

Social studies, which is full of crises, decision-making, problem confrontation, tragedy, and comedy, is a gateway to drama. The purpose of this chapter is to unlock that gate through the use of a variety of dramatic techniques effectively. After a brief descriptive section about the potential role of drama in middle school social studies, we provide a series of activities using different types of drama. In each activity, we give some suggested steps for creating content-appropriate models and illustrate with examples.

Why Drama?

Drama takes two basic forms with shades of combinations. First, there is interpretational drama that begins with the written word that the dramatic player reads or memorizes and recites (Turner, 2013). This drama includes radio scripts, reader's theatre, and skits. Middle school students learn to vary expressions and read with excitement. These types of drama activities develop reading fluency.

Second, there is improvisational drama which begins with some sort of prompt or situation. The students create a script and plot in response (Clabough, Turner, Russell, & Waters, 2016). Examples include role play, socio-drama, and process drama. This type of drama develops problem solving and empathy as students think about what their character would say. The drama itself is created by the actors as they devise their own script.

Variants and combinations of both forms can have great benefits to learning for middle school students. These benefits along with brief explanations of how they occur are shown in Figure 8.1.

Figure 8.1 *Benefits of Drama*

Drama:	It works because it causes students to:
Takes away fears of looking foolish.	Absorb themselves in roles.
Involves problem solving and gets students to think. (O'Neill, 2014)	Work out alternative outcomes, best fit, and arguments.
Is ego gratifying, giving personal satisfaction and confidence.	Find solutions, feel good about their performances, and take on character roles.
Gives purpose and motivation for research.	Learn about roles, character background, and scenario situations

Helps students to learn empathy and sympathy while taking the roles of historical characters.	Look into the feelings and motivation of historical characters.
Helps students learn to articulate their ideas and convince others.	Hide behind roles as they speak, gaining confidence as their ideas are expressed.
Teaches discussion skills.	Learn to dialogue – since drama is essentially idea exchange.

In the remainder of this chapter, we describe four different types of dramatic activities that can be successfully adapted for the middle level. The first three are interpretational. With these activities, only reading is required, with no memorization. This enables students to concentrate more on the performance, since they do not have to study lines. Repeated practice in the reading aloud brings greater smoothness and ability to concentrate on different dramatic expressions and interpretations. The final activity is improvisational in nature and requires students to express ideas and solve problems. Students are not reciting someone else's pre-written script but creating the words as they go.

Brags and Whines: The Great Wall of China

Brags and whines are forms of monologues written and performed in role. A person, place, or thing represents himself, herself, or itself to the world in a presentation aimed at showing character and accomplishments in the most self-justifying way possible. She or he wants to either aggrandize her/himself beyond all believability (brags) or to complain about her/his mistreatment by biographers, historians, and writers (whines) (Turner & Clabough, 2015).

Brags and whines can be prepared in advance by others for students to read aloud, or they can be written by the middle schoolers themselves. The process of writing, in either case, is fairly simple. The writer must first look at some good examples of brags and whines provided by the teacher and then do some research and reading about the subject. The objective of this is twofold: to understand the topic generally and as thoroughly as possible and to accumulate a set of basic facts or quote fragments to work into the brag or whine as it is written. The second step is to write the brag, inserting the findings of the research, adding bits of humor and historical reference, and, keeping the writing tight and terse. The third step is to practice and perform the monologue as dramatically as possible. During this step, the performer should refine and edit the script, often referred to as "smoothing."

An eighth grade teacher in Birmingham, Alabama volunteered to get her students to write some brags and whines in the "person" of the Great Wall of China. Each of the 25 examples she shared with us was interesting in its own right. In the interest of space, we will share two examples.

The first of these is a brag, and the student who wrote it not only shows an understanding of facts about the wall but gives the famous structure attitude and personality. The reader can pick up the comedic style and expressive ability given to the piece by this talented young writer.

Historical Brag for The Great Wall of China

Ni hao, simpletons! I'm The Great Wall of China. That's right, you heard correctly. The Great Wall of China! What makes me so great is that I was built 2,000 years ago and still stand tall to this day! Talk about great, I'm the best! The glorious son of a gun who came up with the idea of me was named Qin Shi Huangdi, and he was a pretty cool dude. I have to say, it's sad that he went to the little China in the sky. However, his work was not in vain. My Ming wall, the part of me that was built by the Ming dynasty during 1368-1644, goes across nine provinces. This includes Liaoning, Tianjin, Beijing, Inner Mongolia, Shanxi, Shaanxi, Ningxia, and Gansu.

Not to toot my own horn or anything, but in December 1987, I was placed on the World Heritage List by UNESCO. I was frequently used during war, and the military always made me feel like I was part of the team, which made this wall pretty happy. Speaking of war, that was one of my uses. I kept barbarians away from China, protecting all of our citizens and our wonderful emperors. Another thing I was used for was keeping the nomads out of precious, sweet China. It needed to be done! Those annoying, trifling nomads… all they do is move from place to place. Like, sit DOWN! Not only that, I kept the Chinese in, so they would never escape, because that would be the ultimate betrayal. After all, we don't need cultural diffusion, because our culture is perfect~ and no one needs to ruin it. Anyway, I forgot about my other name, it's pretty cool. My nickname is Long Graveyard! Isn't that cool!? The reason I'm called that is because during my construction the workers (such lazy people) died of starvation, disease, and heat stroke.

The second young writer chose to take the whine format, including some modern idioms. Emphasis is on the many people who died while building the wall and the disposal of their bodies. There is a sociological concern too with the wall's influence on cultural diffusion.

Historical Whine for the Great Wall of China

I hate being the Great Wall of China. I'm dead on the inside. Literally, I'm dead on the inside. There are dead bodies inside of me. You see, when I was being built, many people couldn't handle the harsh conditions they had to work in. Working hours in the rain, snow, wind, and other weather conditions can take a toll on a person. I really wouldn't know since I'm a wall. From what I saw, humans cannot stand the weather like I can. I saw many humans die and the worst part is when they died, the others just threw them inside of me. Gross, I know! See, I really am dead on the inside.

Another reason I stink is the fact that I prevented cultural diffusion. Yes, I know what cultural diffusion is. Being a wall doesn't mean that I'm a dummy. Since I was built, no new cultures could come in. The Chinese Empire could not grow for many years since I kept the people in. If that is not bad enough, let me tell you about what happened on the inside. I caused China to be like a jail. Well, it was mainly Shi Huangdi, but I played a big role. Many people suffered from being trapped inside of me. I watched from all around China as people were beaten, burned, and even buried alive. There were more punishments that were worse but those are just a few. I feel terrible about all the pain that I caused to the people of China. I'm glad that people enjoy visiting me today, but I can't forget the pain I caused in the past. So, I guess that is all you need to know about me, the so called "great" wall of China.

This brag and whine approach allows students not only to develop reading fluency and expression, but it also can be an important writing activity. It gets students to listen to each other in a reflective and evaluative way. They compare what others have done to their own work and can learn from that. AMLE stresses this type of collaboration is needed among students to build a warm and positive learning environment (NMSA, 2010).

ACTIVITY Anachronistic Phone Call Monologues: Churchill Calling FDR

The anachronistic phone call monologue technique scripts one side of a phone conference. A dialogue is going on between two figures from history but only one side can be heard by the audience. The monologue is "anachronistic" because it occurs at a time when the technology was not yet available (Turner & Clabough, 2015). The teacher can adapt the technique to fit the content being studied. The example that follows is an imaginary talk between Churchill and Roosevelt on

December 9, 1941, before a transatlantic phone cable had been laid (that occurred in the 1950s.). Winston Churchill is the voice that is heard.

Operator: This is London calling. President Roosevelt, will you please hold for Prime Minister Churchill? (Pause) Thank you Mr. President. (Pause.)

Churchill: So good to speak with you, Franklin. Ripping good speech yesterday. If the United States should endure for a thousand years, men will still say, "This was their finest hour." (Pause.)

Churchill: I couldn't have said it better myself, and as Clemmie would be quick to tell you, that is high praise coming from me. But the "date which will live in infamy" phrase, - that was really super! Powerful, powerful stuff. (Pause.)

Churchill: I certainly understand that the Japanese were dreadfully underhanded, Franklin. I must say that that has also been our record with Chancellor Hitler.

Churchill: I must add…welcome to our war, Mr. President. Now, let's get to business, shall we? You give us the tools, and we will finish the job. If I may be so crass, Franklin, when may we expect the arrival of American troops, tanks, planes, and ships? (Pause.)

Churchill: Why of course, I will take a ship for the United States at the first opportunity. I shall be there by Christmas, in fact. (Pause.)

Churchill: Of course, I would be more than delighted to address Congress. Shall we say, Boxing Day? (Pause.)

Churchill: Yes, I mean the day after Christmas. Now about those troops, tanks, and ships. (Pause.)

Churchill: Capital! As I have said before, in war, resolution; in defeat, defiance; in victory, magnanimity. Success consists of going from failure to failure without loss of enthusiasm. The Germans have received back from us again that measure of fire and steel which they have so often meted out to others. (Pause.)

Churchill: So very good to speak with you, Franklin. God speed to you. I'll see you in a fortnight.

This approach helps humanize history by including elements of the speaker and the person that he or she is speaking to. The vulnerability and hopes of the speaker shines through his or her words. The students must remember that the speakers are ignorant of the history that follows. In the example here, neither Churchill nor FDR are aware that the Allies would go on to victory in World War II. The anachronistic phone call allows students to explore the perspectives of historical figures, looking through their eyes (NMSA, 2010).

 ## Scandals: The Rascally Dolly Madison

A scandal is a scripted monologue, which takes the events in the life of a historical character and reports them as though they were malicious gossip. With this activity, students can write their own script or perform someone else's scripted scandals as though they were announcers on a TV show. In order to write a scandal, they need to first have read at least one example as a model. We have suggested several steps in the process below.

1. Take known and innocent events, even great accomplishments in a person's life, and turn it into a scandal.

2. Use lots of big words that seem like accusations.

3. Tell the story with attitude and expression that hints of intrigue and hidden secrets.

4. Misconstrue the meaning of acts.

Following these steps can enable teachers and students to write their own scandals. We have provided an example in the next section about a scandal concerning Dolly Madison.

Have You Heard the Dirt on Dolly Madison

This reporter has an exclusive on a new White House scandal. Our President's wife, Dolly Madison, was seen today removing paintings and other treasures from the White House and then fleeing Washington. Included among the things that Mrs. Madison removed was the famous portrait of our beloved first president, George Washington. Has this woman no sense of history at all? It can only be speculated that our First Lady's lavish and extravagant parties have made her so desperate for money that she is seeking to sell off our heritage in order to pay for her wasteful lifestyle. A later report from a very reliable source was that the White House and much of the surrounding are now burning. Is this criminal only trying to cover up her crime? The American people need to know.

Scandal writing helps students realize the purpose of point of view. Different writers can construe facts in different ways to either lionize or vilify historical figures. Understanding this in turn helps students to see how words can be manipulated to ruin reputations or to build them. Students need to realize that what politicians do and say is often twisted by their opponents as well their supporters. This is important for students as they become voters and citizens to make informed decisions (NMSA, 2010).

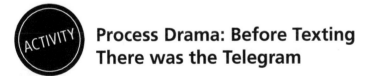

Process Drama: Before Texting There was the Telegram

Process drama is unique in that it was conceived and developed as a teaching approach in which students learn problem solving skills (Bolton & Heathcote, 1995). Elements of process learning have since been used by innovators in social studies including Margit McGuire, developer of the Storypath approach (McGuire, 2008). The essential thing to remember about drama in general and process drama in particular is that drama has to have content (Powell & Heap, 2013). This means, in effect, that the social studies are well served by process drama. It also means that careful planning is necessary. The teacher has to think out the sequence of the drama, the roles that students play and their relevancy, and the questions and problems that the students as participants must consider.

The following example of process drama relates to America's entry into what was originally referred to as the "Great War" and is now called World War I. It particularly focuses on the Zimmermann Telegram and encoded message sent by German Foreign Secretary Arthur Zimmermann to the German Ambassador to Mexico.

Prior to the drama session, the teacher and students need to explore the "Great War," its importance, and the events leading up to it. The impact of submarines on the style of the war and the impact that German U-Boats had on British rule of the seas should be part of that discussion. For the drama, students should be divided into four groups, one smaller than the others. Each group can discuss roles they want to play as individuals. To make the process more effective, the teacher will probably want to assign key roles in each group. The chart in Figure 8.2 shows what some of these roles might be.

Figure 8.2 *Suggested Roles for the Process Drama*

England	David Lloyd George—Prime Minister
	Sir George Cave—Home Secretary
	Arthur Balfour—Foreign Secretary
	British Code Breakers (allow multiple students to participate here)
	*Note: The British depended a lot on American goods.

United States	Woodrow Wilson—President
	Newton D. Baker—Secretary of War
	Robert Lansing—Secretary of War
	Walter Hines Page—U.S. Ambassador to Britain
	Key members of the American public (allow multiple students to participate here)
	*Note: America shared a language and a history with Britain. However, there was some resentment of the British colonial attitude toward the United States. There were also lots of German immigrants and German sympathy among Americans. President Wilson's second election campaign used the slogan, "He kept us out of war."
Germany	Arthur Zimmermann—Foreign Secretary of the German Empire
	Heinrich von Eckhardt—German Ambassador to Mexico
	German Leaders including Kaiser Wilhelm II (allow multiple students to participate here)
	*Note: Germany was hopeful that the U.S. could be kept out of the war. However, their strategy was to isolate England from receiving supplies and war materials. They believed that American ships, including passenger vessels, were secretly bringing weapons and ammunition
Mexico	Venustiano Carranza—President of Mexico
	Candido Aguilar—Foreign Secretary of Mexico
	Victoriano Huerto—Exiled former Mexican President courted by German Agents in exchange for help in ousting Carranza.
	The Mexican public (allow multiple students to participate here)
	*Note: The Mexican government had been in turmoil for some time prior to this, and there had been nine declared presidents since 1911.

It should be noted that the first step in the drama process is that everyone must have a role, regardless of how minor. Minor players may alter their roles as the drama develops. This activity unfolds in three drama events. Each event consists of three segments: an introduction of the situation and problem, a dramatized discussion with each group in succession, and a debriefing discussion involving the entire class. Every student needs to be made aware of the importance of his or her acting role and audience role. Figure 8.3 shows the three drama events and includes group tasks and resources.

Figure 8.3 *America's Entry into the "Great War" Drama Events*

First Drama Event	The various groups discuss the impact of unrestricted submarine warfare.
	On February 4, 1915, the Germans declared unrestricted submarine warfare in the North Sea. In May 1915, the RMS Lusitania was torpedoed and sunk along with several other American ships in British waters. What was the American reaction? President Wilson's protest is found online at *http://www.firstworldwar.com/source/bryanlusitaniaprotest.htm*.
	Public response in America can be seen on the front page of the *New York Tribune* found online at *http://chroniclingamerica.loc.gov/lccn/sn83030214/1915-05-08/ed-1/seq-1/#words=l.usitania+Lusitania+LUSITANIA*.
	How did the Germans explain their reasons for the decision and what consequences did they expect?
	How did the British use these events to garner American support?

Second Drama Event	On January 29,1917, German Foreign Secretary Zimmermann sent a telegram to German Ambassador to Mexico. The Zimmermann Telegram can be found online at
	https://www.archives.gov/education/lessons/zimmermann. The British intercepted this telegram and shared it with the Americans. The various groups deal with their reasoning in this step of the dramatic activity.
	The Germans review their reasons for the telegram and their hopes.
	The British discuss their hopes and goals in sharing the telegram with the Americans.
	The Mexicans lay out their reactions to the proposal and the reasons behind them.
	The Americans consider why they first thought the telegram was a forgery and how they reacted once they realized it was genuine.
	On February 3, 1917, the United States severs diplomatic ties with Germany after a U-Boat sinks the American grain ship *Housatonic*. Seven more American ships are sunk in February and March.
Third Drama Event	On April 2, 1917 - President Woodrow Wilson appeared before the U.S. Congress and gave a speech saying "the world must be made safe for democracy" then asked Congress for a declaration of war against Germany. On April 6, 1917, the United States of America declared war on Germany. All of the groups consider the impact of this event.
	The British describe their reactions.
	The Americans consider their reasons for entering the European war.
	The Germans evaluate their expectation and the impact they anticipate of America's entry into the "Great War."

Process drama allows students to enter history through the eyes of the characters that were there (Kelley, 2006). It brings reality and humanity to events and characters and provides students with unique insights and perspectives about the "Great War" that are real and vital. History becomes a problem-solving experience rather than a mere memorization of dry facts. It invites deep learning and gives a much needed excitement and motivation to do probing research. Activities such as process drama show students the interconnectedness of the world through history. Earth is a global village (NMSA, 2010).

Conclusion

The brief description of the use of drama and the examples offered in this chapter just scratches the surface of the opportunities for drama in the middle school. Drama takes many other forms, most of them beneficial for students of all ages. Monologues and conflict dramas alone could fill several volumes. Drama is important to the social studies because it teaches the process of problem solving and can be used to learn and reflect on history, culture, and current affairs (Clabough, Turner, Russell, & Waters, 2016). It gives middle level students new eyes to see the world past and present. Through drama, students can gain perspectives on history and culture that can be learned in no other way. Drama also can inspire students to research the roles they take and the events they portray as no other motivation can do. Drama is most definitely a learning medium. Ultimately, middle schoolers become excited about learning, learn facts because they need them rather than for a test, and become self-motivated.

Additional Drama Activities

1. Have students dramatize a historical novel or biography. In order to do this, students will need to first discuss the book and then nominate and choose the critical incidents that best represent the plot line of the story. They need to organize the drama by deciding who will play the critical characters and then outline the discussion segments. One good example might be *Good Masters! Sweet Ladies!:Voices from a Medieval Village* (Schlitz, 2011). This book is essentially a series of descriptions of some of the key types of people in a medieval village and has no real plot per se. It would be dramatized as a series of brief monologues with a common theme.
Schlitz, L. (2011). *Good masters! sweet ladies!: Voices from a medieval village.* Cambridge, MA: Candlewick Press.

2. Have students deliver book reports of biographies of historical personages in first person. They would need to portray three or more life events in detail. This means that they have to empathize with the lead character in the book and be very expressive in talking about life events.

3. Students can learn a lot about a culture by dramatizing one or more of its celebrations, rituals, and customs. For example, they may present a normal or special event meal. This may be done in improvised or scripted conversations among the characters at the meal, or a narrator may describe the events as the other students enact them in pantomime.

4. Students can create scripted representations of meetings between famous historical characters. These may be their researched idea of meetings that actually occurred like the Yalta Conference among Ally leaders in 1945 or the first meeting of Washington and Lafayette. Alternatively, they can present their idea of meetings that never really occurred among contemporary characters. For example, they might have a "Wives' Club Meeting" for the spouses of the Framers of the Constitution.

5. Students can create marketplace and meeting events from history like a Greek agora, a Roman Forum, a medieval fair, or a Middle Eastern bazaar. To do this, they need to research the kinds of goods that might be bought and sold and find out the elements in bargaining and exchange. The middle schoolers can then use their research to determine their roles and set up dialogue.

References

Bolton, G. & Heathcote, D. (1995). *Drama for learning: Dorothy Heathcote's mantle of the expert approach to education.* Portsmouth, NH: Heinemann.

Clabough, J., Turner, T., Russell, W., & Waters, S. (2016). *Unpuzzling history with primary sources.* Charlotte, NC: Information Age Publishing.

Kelley, K. (2006). "I'm not like her": Entering the world of others thorough process drama. In Schneider, J. J., Crumple, T.P., & Rogers, Theresa (Eds.), *Process drama and multiple literacies* (71-87). Portsmouth, NH: Heinemann.

McGuire, M. (2008). Using the storypath approach to make local governments understandable. *The Social Studies, 99*(2), 85-90.

NMSA. (2010). *This we believe: Keys to educating young adolescents.* Westerville, OH: Author.

O'Neill, C. (2014). *Dorothy Heathcote on education and drama: Essential writings.* New York, NY: Routledge.

Powell, P. & Heap, B. (2013). *Planning process drama: Enriching teaching and learning* (2nd ed.). New York, NY: Routledge.

Turner, T. (2013). The play's the thing: Integrating drama with social studies. In T. Lintner (Ed.), *Integrative strategies for the K-12 social studies classroom* (39-61). Charlotte, NC: Information Age Publishing.

Turner, T. & Clabough, J. (2015). Dramatic social studies monologues to stir the gifted soul. *Teaching for High Potential,* 14-16.

09

"Laboratory for Democracy": No Robots Need Apply

Thomas Jefferson and John Dewey are among the many Americans who have stressed the purpose of schools is to prepare students to assume the role of being a democratic citizen (Barr, Barth, & Shermis, 1977). A special mindset is needed to be an effective citizen in a democracy. Most importantly, it requires students to realize that they must be part of the solution to the problems of a society. The National Council for the Social Studies (NCSS) stresses that students must take action to improve their communities and the nation (NCSS, 2013a). Middle school teachers need to prepare students to be effective citizens. What they do to achieve this is referred to as a citizenship education program.

Being a citizen in a democracy is neither easy nor simple. Democratic citizenship comes with responsibilities. Good citizens are not only voters, but they hold elected officials accountable for their words and actions. They must be the guardians of the democracy. As Jefferson said, "An enlightened citizenry is indispensable for the proper functioning of a republic" (n.d.).

This chapter is about aspects of citizenship education that should be included in a middle school program. In reality, it is all about building civic identity. Therefore, we start with a brief discussion about the purposes for citizenship education highlighted in the C3 Framework. Next, we shift to the idea that middle school social studies classrooms should become "laboratories for democracy" where students think about solutions to problems and apply democratic concepts and principles to contemporary issues. A list of key components to create a "laboratory for democracy" is provided. Four activities are offered that connect to several of these components of a "laboratory of democracy" as well as AMLE's *This We Believe* (NMSA, 2010). An appendix is included that connects additional activities to the concept of a "laboratory of democracy."

Connections Between Citizenship Education and Education Reform Movements

The major goal of current education reform movements is to promote content-area literacy skills. For social studies, this means that students can analyze and articulate the ideas, perspectives, values, beliefs, and biases of an individual from a text (Clabough, Turner, Russell, & Waters, 2016). The C3 Framework stresses this goal, as seen in the disciplinary standards and inquiry arc. However, it goes one step farther. Dimension four of the inquiry arc stresses that after students complete analyses of open-ended questions they need to take civic action (NCSS, 2013b). Some examples of civic action include participating in town hall meetings to support policy helpful for a local community, working as a volunteer for the campaign of a political candidate, or organizing community-wide efforts to solve local problems.

Current education reform in social studies emphasizes students developing the ability to critically explore issues and public policies in depth and then create solutions to contemporary and historical issues. Social studies teachers need to embrace discussions of contemporary issues, even those that can be controversial. Our perceptions of public policies are influenced by our social, cultural, geographical, and religious values and beliefs. People have different values and beliefs (Nokes, 2013). This means that students need to deal with disagreements. Disagreements can be healthy for a democracy if people listen to one another and use discussion as the basis for negotiated solutions to problems (Hess, 2009).

Problems Within Contemporary American Politics

American politics today is a barroom brawl. There are no rules of honesty, ethics, or fairness. No politician is offering workable solutions. This political climate is unhealthy for the vitality and longevity of a democracy.

What can a 12-year-old do about it? That is what civic education is about in our middle schools. Civics in our schools must be more than having students memorize vocabulary terms in our state standards. Students need to consider how they should use these terms. For example, "yelling it is a free country" does not even compare to understanding what the Bill of Rights or the concept of checks and balances really means.

Our social studies classrooms should focus on creating "laboratories for democracy." Teachers need to use activities that enable students to apply democratic principles to solve contemporary and historical issues (Clabough & Wooten, 2016). For example, students may look at issues such as immigration, the national debt, and unemployment. They need to use the analysis skills contained within the C3 Framework. Students need to be respectful of others' opinions, even if they disagree, when sharing their solutions and use evidence from sources to support their arguments. AMLE stresses that teachers need to create an environment where students feel safe to share and discuss their opinions (NMSA, 2010).

So how do we create a "laboratory for democracy?" We have provided a list of components that are needed for a social studies classroom to become a "laboratory of democracy" below.

1. Students should learn and understand the rights and responsibilities of being a citizen in different systems of government.

2. Students must be able to decode the messages in political candidates' speeches to make informed decisions.

3. Students need to understand how they can effectively and actively participate in shaping public policy at local, state, and federal levels.

4. Students need to learn by doing that, in a democracy, individual service can have a positive impact on people.

5. Students need to learn how to discuss, debate, and deliberate in a civil manner.

6. Students need to learn how to cooperate with one another in equitable ways.

7. Students need to learn how to use active listening skills.

8. Students should learn to make their points clearly and distinctly in speaking.

9. Students should be able to distinguish justice from injustice and know how to deal with injustices.

10. Students should learn to tirelessly advocate for their beliefs.

Our list is far from exhaustive but does provide direction for how we envision citizenship education in middle schools. The activities that follow and the appendix attempt to practically implement these precepts.

Teaching Students about Citizens' Rights and Responsibilities in Systems of Government

ACTIVITY

Many students know little and understand less about their government. The complexity of government and distorted impressions given by the media and politicians contribute to this. Students do not often realize that their tax dollars help repair roads, pay police officers and firefighters, fund public schools and hospitals, maintain state parks, provide funds for Medicare and Medicaid, and support the financial needs of colleges. Schools are responsible for ensuring that students understand all of this. In order for students to explore and examine issues in a "laboratory of democracy," they need to have a basic understanding of different types of government. This understanding helps them take on their roles as future citizens. Here is one activity by which teachers can enable students to understand some of the functions of government as well as their rights and responsibilities as citizens.

In this activity, students examine the different roles and responsibilities of citizens in the three basic types of government—democracy, oligarchy, and dictatorship—by completing a compare and contrast diagram (see Figure 9.1). They complete the compare and contrast diagram in groups of three using the jigsaw approach. Jigsaw involves each student as a contributor with a part of the solution to a problem. Each member of the initial group joins one of three expert groups to look at the questions in the diagram for one of the types of government.

Figure 9.1 *Compare and Contrast Diagram for Types of Government*

Types of Government	Democracy	Oligarchy	Dictatorship
How can citizens petition their leaders about an issue?			
In what ways can citizens protest public policies?			
What is the role of the military in the system of government?			
How is the leader of the government chosen for a country?			
What is the role of the government in terms of public services?			

After expert groups complete the questions for their assigned type of government, they return to their initial group and share findings. This allows the students to become experts on a topic and teach their peers. The teacher should float around the room to answer and clarify any items during this sharing. Students fill in the diagram from peers' comments. The teacher then brings the class together to discuss their diagrams, clarifying any questions. After this debriefing, students use information from the diagram and class discussion to write a short letter as a citizen in one of three forms of government discussed to petition a leader about an issue. The letter needs to contain evidence showing that students grasp the powers and limitations of being a citizen in a particular form of government. The length of this letter should be a half-page to a page.

This activity gets students to think about the roles and responsibilities of citizens. Students apply their comparisons in the diagram to complete the letter. Social studies classrooms can be a place where students can think about governments in an objective manner. The understandings that they gain help them not only be better citizens in their own system of government but also better grasp other systems of government (NMSA, 2010).

ACTIVITY: Analyzing Political Messages by Candidates and Decoding the Layers of Meaning

Politicians try to inspire voters to support them using national pride, shared values and ideas, and other types of propaganda techniques. This kind of persuasive language is magnified in presidential elections. Successful candidates thoughtfully and purposefully speak to the political, social, cultural, and economic values of the American people (Journell, 2013). Their speeches, statements, and commercials become a window into the issues and events of the era. Students need to analyze such political messages in our social studies classrooms to experiment with and form their civic identities.

For this activity, students examine the nomination speech and inaugural address of Richard Nixon during the 1968 presidential election. We choose Nixon because of his impact on shaping the modern composition of both the Republican and Democratic parties (Perlstein, 2009). The teacher may have students, in pairs, look at either

Nixon's nomination speech or inaugural address. Both of these documents can be accessed from The American Presidency Project, *http://www.presidency.ucsb.edu/ index.php*. Each pair should complete the questions on the analysis sheet provided here. These questions help students explore Nixon's political tactics for his 1968 Inaugural Address.

- How does Nixon address contemporary issues, and what do his solutions say about his beliefs, values, and biases?

- What is one issue that Nixon discusses, and how was the language of his speech designed to emotionally impact the voters?

- How do the issues that he discusses appeal to the values, beliefs, biases, and hopes of Republican voters?

After reading their assigned speech, have the students complete the analysis sheet (see Figure 9.2). The teacher will guide the class through a debriefing. Students need to complete the two-sided analysis sheet while listening to their peers' comments. The teacher should ask students about how Nixon appeals through his language to voters in these two documents. This allows the teacher to help students understand how politicians prey on people's fears, biases, and prejudices. Students' ability to detect such negative tactics enables them to deal better with political messages (NCSS, 2013a).

The teacher then asks students to examine a set of quotes from Richard Nixon. From the speech that students are studying, they list specific quotes in the first column. Students discuss the meaning of the quote in the second column and then analyze his reasons for specific language in the third column. The completion of this chart enables students to see how political candidates use language to influence the voters' feelings and perceptions about issues. An example of how this sheet might look follows.

Figure 9.2 *Quote Analysis Sheet*

Nixon Quote	The Meaning of This Quote	Why Did He Say This?
"We are going to win because this great Convention has demonstrated to the nation that the Republican Party has the leadership, the platform, and the purpose that America needs."	Nixon is trying to convince undecided voters that the Republican Party has the answers to problems in this country.	Nixon is subtly implying that the Democratic Party is lacking in leadership and purpose to meet the challenges in the United States.
"The choice we make in 1968 will determine not only the future of America but the future of peace and freedom in the world for the last third of the twentieth century."	Nixon is suggesting that the person elected will be responsible for handling conflicts like the Vietnam War.	Nixon is trying to convince people that he is best suited to deal with bringing and preserving peace.
"It is another voice. It is the quiet voice in the tumult and the shouting. It is the voice of the great majority of Americans, the forgotten Americans—the non-shouters; the non-demonstrators."	Nixon claims that the majority of voters are not active participants in the protests. This group was referred to as the "Silent Majority."	Nixon wants to attract the "Silent Majority" and, with their help, rebuild the nation.
"When the nation with the greatest tradition of the rule of law is plagued by unprecedented lawlessness"	Nixon wants the people to see him as the candidate that will bring law and order back.	Nixon wants to convince voters that activism by Democrats has caused the deterioration of law and order resulting in increased crime.

This activity can be used with any presidential election cycle. It enables students to see how candidates craft and hone their messages to appeal to the voters. This analysis of specific language allows students to evaluate a candidate's strengths and weaknesses. Students learn skills that allow them to hold candidates accountable for misspeaks, distortions, and lies (NMSA, 2010). These political tactics are toxic to the vitality of healthy political discourse. This is the level of civic activism that is needed from citizens in a democracy (Levine, 2007).

Laws: The Bare Bones of Building Public Policy

Laws are the skeleton that supports policies that impact us all. The passage of social security helped provide some financial stability for many; the 1965 Civil Rights Voting Act was a lethal blow to Jim Crow segregation; and the Federal-Aid Highway Act of 1956 moved the country toward a federal interstate system. Citizens should not be passive about public policies instituted at any level. Good citizenship encourages students to be actively involved. Middle school students need to dive into public policies to see possible positive and negative ramifications. They need to be able to put their reasoning into words. This process reflects the experimental nature of a democracy, in that citizens and politicians do not know what the outcome of public policies will be. Good citizens will use the best available evidence to formulate their best hypothesis about which policies need to be supported and enacted.

In this activity, students complete an in-basket simulation related to various policies enacted in a state. In-basket simulations are priority-setting activities that ask students to rank order items based on priority (Cole, 2015). In this case, the scenario includes 10 possible policies. The students in groups of three should order the 10 items based on how much they will help the state. Each group then selects their highest priority item and writes a paragraph explaining their reasoning (see Figure 9.3).

Figure 9.3 *In-Basket Simulation for State Public Policy*

Bill One	authorizes spending a significant amount of state funds to bring a major company into an underfunded area of the state. This would bring a little over 200 jobs into a city. The problem is that the company is not willing to sign a contract longer than three years.
Bill Two	is to maintain and repair your state roads. This bill will lead to an increased employment of construction workers in the state for this job and improve transportation in the state.
Bill Three	addresses skyrocketing health care costs. This bill would raise the amount of state spending for citizens on Medicare and Medicaid. However, it does not pay for all of the medical costs.
Bill Four	addresses rising crime rates in three major cities by providing more funds for police officers but only in these three cities.
Bill Five	gives teachers in the state a 2% salary raise. There have been no raises for teachers in five years. It would result in a tax increase on all citizens in the state. However, able teachers are already leaving the state in large numbers.
Bill Six	funds the renovation of state parks. Without this expenditure, the parks will probably lose attendance and reduce their appeal to out of state tourists. This plan would modernize all of the parks. However, this policy does not create new jobs and will be time consuming to carry out.
Bill Seven	authorizes spending to digitize all state records. This would make it easier to access and store the records of the state and result in the creation of about 50 new jobs. One problem is that the state will also have to purchase new equipment for the changeover.
Bill Eight	authorizes more spending for state colleges and universities. This is needed for maintenance, pay raises, and funding for research. This funding could result in more student enrollment and new companies coming into some of your communities.

Figure 9.3 (continued) *In-Basket Simulation for State Public Policy*

Bill Nine	delegates state funds to build a new stadium for a professional sports team. The cost to the state may be as high as 25% of the state budget. Team owners are threatening to move their franchise to another state. That would hurt the overall revenue of the city where the team is located and the state through merchandise sales.
Bill Ten	raises the state minimum wage from seven dollars an hour to ten dollars an hour. This policy aims to help the working class in your state but may lead to inflation costs on goods. Additionally, several companies have already stated that they will have to lay off a lot of workers if this policy is implemented.

In both group and class discussion, students need to consider the positive and negative ramifications of each bill. The teacher should encourage students to dig as deeply as possible. After the students discuss the options in groups, have them share their reasoning as a class. This provides students the opportunity to formulate and articulate arguments for public policies with evidence (Engle & Ochoa, 1988). Students need to discuss how they will deal with the limitations and problems with their selected item.

This activity prepares students for their future role of impacting public policy on the state level. Students must weigh the pros and cons of public policies and then decide the legislation that they wish to support (Engle, 1960). Through this activity, they may realize some of the limitations of a state budget. This builds their problem solving and decision making skills in the process (NMSA, 2010).

Using Service-Learning Projects for Stronger Student Engagement

Current technological advances have created a society that is more mobile than previous generations. One of the negative repercussions of this is that people's lives are often fragmented. People may work in one location, engage in recreational activities in others, and finally live in another part of a city. They are often disconnected from their local communities. Service-learning projects can help students be involved. Through student involvement in service-learning projects, middle schoolers can begin to see how they can have an impact for a positive change in society.

Service-learning projects are designed to get students to problem solve in their own neighborhood (Cipolle, 2010). For example, students may volunteer at a food kitchen, donate canned foods to Second Harvest, and contribute in a beautification project in a community. The teacher will want to initially brainstorm a list of possible projects and organizations to partner with based on the needs of a local community. For service-learning projects to work, it is important for the teacher to first explain their importance. The teacher should start off with small projects. Students need to understand not only the purpose of the project and the steps necessary to perform it but also the appropriate behavior while working within a community.

One approach to building relationships with organizations to carry out service-learning projects involves the education staff at Vulcan Park and Museum. Vulcan Park and Museum is home to the world's largest cast iron statue and a center that focuses on local history of the Birmingham area, *http://visitvulcan.com*. Like most historic sites and parks, the museum can use volunteer help. Even middle schoolers can engage in service learning projects there. For example, they could work at Vulcan Park and Museum on beautification projects, volunteer at community events held on-site, and assist and mentor other children during summer camp projects. After any service-learning project, the teacher needs to guide a class debriefing that focuses on getting students to assess the impact they had on their communities and future projects that could be completed (Meaney, Kent, & Bohler, 2009). The teacher may use some of the following questions during this class debriefing.

- Who benefited from our project?
- In what ways did the project help people in our community?
- How did the completion of our project make you feel?
- What are some future projects that we could do in our community, and why should we complete these items?

A larger service-learning project involves students constructing a play about the history of Birmingham and presenting it to members of the community. Middle school students could focus on the iron industry, music in the area during the Great Depression, the city's role during World War II, and the pivotal events of the Civil Rights Movement in Birmingham. The project obviously involves preparation such as research activities, script writing and editing, casting and rehearsals, and working with the community to advertise the project. All large service-learning projects involve the teacher building a strong working relationship between the school and partner organization. The teacher also needs to make the project doable by segmenting it into manageable chunks. Such a service-learning project will make the site more visible to the community, build social concern in the students, and develop a sense of community for all involved.

Service-learning projects encourage students to invest in their own community. They are active change agents meeting the needs of their fellow citizens (Wade, 2011). These projects make social studies concrete and relevant to our students (NMSA, 2010). Students gain sympathy and empathy for the people in their neighborhoods.

At the completion of a project, they leave with a feeling of satisfaction that their actions had a positive impact on their communities. This increases the likelihood that students will engage in future service-learning projects (Bringle, Clayton, & Hatcher 2013).

Conclusion

Students' identities are largely shaped during their time in middle school (NMSA, 2010). Middle school curricula should be structured to build students' identities as citizens, with the dispositions, values, and beliefs to be actively engaged in a democracy. We have suggested approaches in this chapter that can make middle school social studies classrooms "laboratories of democracy" where students can explore, examine, and offer solutions to contemporary issues. Through the four model activities discussed and those found in the additional activities section of this chapter, students practice some of the future skills needed to be active stakeholders in this country. All of these activities imply a high level of activism, which is absolutely necessary for the continued vitality of a democracy.

Additional Activities for Creating "Laboratories of Democracy"

1. One website to help students build their civic identity is iCivics, *https://www.icivics.org*. There they can do the "The Candidate Evaluation Activity" *(https://www.icivics.org/teachers/lesson-plans/candidate-evaluation)*. This activity lets students explore issues in-depth and discuss their political values.

2. Students need to research and discuss historical injustices. One ideal example is McCarthyism. This topic allows students to discuss the ability to object to undemocratic practices. Students can then create historical memes using *http://imgur.com* to discuss the injustices of McCarthyism. A historical meme is simply using a photograph or drawing with a caption to convey an idea or

emotional reaction. A "director's cut" needs to be included where students discuss the content of their historical meme along with the symbolism and ideas embedded in their image. The length of this "director's cut" should be a paragraph. The components of this activity enable students to articulate the reasons that certain events are injustices in a democratic society.

3. Students need to engage in deliberation to explore and reach solutions about contemporary issues. For example, they may research different solutions to the national debt and weigh the merits and weaknesses of each plan. The teacher then guides a deliberation about strengths and weaknesses of each solution to the national debt. The students then decide on the best option to implement of these plans. More information about deliberation can be gained from reviewing the website of the Kettering Foundation, *https://www.kettering.org/shared-learning/research-positions*.

4. Students need to find issues that are important to them and advocate for these causes. The teacher should have students research one contemporary issue that they want to advocate for and come up with a plan to bring attention to this issue. Some example issues may include entitlement reform, illegal immigration, term limits for elected representatives, and restructuring the tax code. This activity enables students to gain experience advocating for an issue.

5. Students are exposed to many advertisements during each presidential cycle. They need to be able to analyze the messages within these advertisements. The teacher can use Living Room Candidate, *http://www.livingroomcandidate.org*, for this critical examination. The 1964 presidential election is ideal for this activity because it established many of the propaganda techniques used by both major political parties. Students may explore and discuss the propaganda techniques in LBJ and Goldwater's commercials. Some items that they can examine include bandwagoning, fear tactics, mudslinging against your rival, and dramatic imagery.

References

Barr, R., Barth, J., & Shermis, S. (1977). *Defining the social studies.* The National Council for the Social Studies. Bulletin 51. Silver Spring, MD: NCSS.

Bringle, R., Clayton, P., & Hatcher, Julie. (2013). Research on service learning: An introduction. In P. Clayton, R. Bringle, & J. Hatcher (Eds.), *Research on service learning: Conceptual frameworks and assessment* (3-25). Sterling, VA: Stylus Publishing.

Cipolle, S. (2010). *Service-learning and social justice: Engaging students in social change.* Lanham, MD: Rowman & Littlefield Education.

Clabough, J., Turner, T., Russell, W., & Waters, S. (2016). *Unpuzzling history with primary sources.* Charlotte, NC: Information Age Publishing.

Clabough, J. & Wooten, D. (2016). Bias, bigotry, and bungling: Teaching about the Port Chicago 50. *Social Education, 80*(3), 160-165.

Cole, W. (2015). Getting to the "core" of the problem: Decision-making activities and Common Core Standards. In T. Turner, J. Clabough, & W. Cole (Eds.), *Getting at the core of the Common Core with social studies* (41-52). Charlotte, NC: Information Age Publishing.

Engle, S. (1960). Decision making: The heart of the social studies. *Social Education,24*(7), 301–306.

Engle, S. & Ochoa, A. (1988). *Education for democratic citizenship: Decision making in the social studies.* New York, NY: Teachers College Press.

Hess, D. (2009). *Controversy in the classroom: The democratic power of discussion.* New York, NY: Routledge.

Jefferson, T. (n.d.). Retrieved from https://www.monticello.org/site/jefferson/educated-citizenry-vital-requisite-our-survival-free-people-quotation.

Journell, W. (2013). What preservice social studies teachers (don't) know about politics and current events—And why it matters. *Theory & Research in Social Education, 41*(3), 316-351.

Levine, P. (2007). *The future of democracy: Developing the next generation of American citizens.* Medford, MA: Tufts University Press.

Meaney, K. , Kent G., & Bohler, H. (2009). Service learning: A venue for enhancing pre-service educators knowledge based teaching. *International Journal for the Scholarship of Teaching and Learning, 3*(.2), 1-17.

NCSS. (2013a). *Revitalizing civic learning in our schools.* Retrieved from http://www.socialstudies.org/positions/revitalizing_civic_learning.

NCSS. (2013b). *The college, career, and civic life (C3) framework for social studies state standards: Guidance for enhancing the rigor of K-12 civics, economics, geography, and history.* Retrieved from http://socialstudies.org/c3.

NMSA. (2010). *This we believe: Keys to educating young adolescents.* Westerville, OH: Author.

Nokes, J. (2013). *Building students' historical literacies: Learning to read and reason with historical texts and evidence.* New York, NY: Routledge.

Perlstein, R. (2009). *Nixonland: The rise of a president and the fracturing of America.* New York, NY: Scribner.

Wade, R. (2011). Service for learning. *Educational Leadership, 68*(5), 28-31.

Afterword

We are in an age of education reform. Any movement to improve education will impact social studies and its teaching in important and specific ways. The key is finding the best ways to respond to education reform movements in our middle schools. Too often politically motivated reform becomes a witch hunt. Since we start out to find the flaws and faults, we find them, but we find nothing else. The end result is demoralization of teachers, dehumanization of teaching, and defeat of positive change. Schools do not have to be this way. What we want is excited and engaged teachers and students. We do not need new containers for old ideas and labels. Instead, our teaching needs to be recharged, and teachers need real ownership of the reform.

Any education reform movement changes the view of what constitutes best teaching practices. We have highlighted some of the changes implicit in the C3 Framework by the National Council for the Social Studies. We have also provided strategies for teachers to use to meet these more rigorous expectations. The heart of this shift in teaching social studies is the emphasis on student-centered learning. Students need to be actively involved in all steps of the learning process by analyzing evidence to answer open-ended questions, developing their political identities by examining messages of social, cultural, and political groups, and strengthening their content-area literacy skills by scrutinizing and analyzing primary sources. All of these skills engage students in more depth in our content and, more importantly, equip them with the necessary skills to be successful in their careers and as citizens.

No reform movement will really work unless teachers buy into it. Teachers need to think that it is worth their investment in time and energy. They need to genuinely believe that reform will result in more effective classrooms, highly-motivated learners, and greater rewards from teaching. This happens when social studies teachers are designing more engaging, exciting, and energizing activities and assessments. When teachers' creativity is unleashed with their planning, there are no limits to what they can accomplish. This means that it is okay if some of the activities that you envision as masterpieces fall flat. Teachers and students are allowed to experiment. They can do both the "same and new stuff" in different ways. Teachers need to be reflective and analytical about the relative impact of activities and assessments on student learning.

Being an effective social studies teacher is not easy. However, it should not require more time and effort than teachers are already exerting. What teachers do need to do is work smarter on things that they think are more important. The only way that schools can possibly achieve this kind of reform is to create a new focus by school administrations, the general public, and teachers on a positive mindset. Remember that schools, in many respects, are reflections of a society and local community. Many of our students live in poverty, broken families, and in an unsupportive environment for learning. Teachers often feel undervalued, underpaid, and oppressed by imposed restrictions and demands. Even so, the educational community must focus on making schools a positive, safe, and exciting environment where teachers and students are optimists rather than pessimists. Being a middle school social studies teacher is literally full of challenges and opportunities. Winston Churchill reminds us that, "A pessimist sees the difficulty in every opportunity; an optimist sees the opportunity in every difficulty (n.d.)".

References

Churchill, W. (n.d.). Retrieved from http://www.brainyquote.com/quotes/quotes/w/
    winstonchu156899.html.

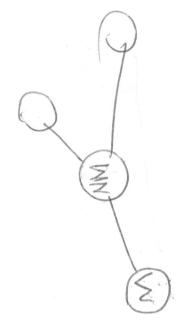

CPSIA information can be obtained
at www.ICGtesting.com
Printed in the USA
LVHW021529151221
706122LV00002B/6

9 781560 902874